IN HOSPITAL ENVIRONMENTS

Essays on Illness and Philosophy

JAKE GOLDSMITH

With Illustrations by Wend Rend

© 2021–2024 by Jake Goldsmith

All Rights Reserved.

Set in Trump Mediaeval with LaTeX.

ISBN: 978-1-952386-93-0 (paperback)
ISBN: 978-1-952386-94-7 (ebook)
Library of Congress Control Number: 2024933379

Sagging Meniscus Press
Montclair, New Jersey
saggingmeniscus.com

for Lemons

A Note on the Author

Jake and I met at school, where he was broadly known for being what he is now: a very distinctive type of person. He showed little interest in formal education, and preferred to pursue his own curriculum, which revolved mainly around literature, ornithology, and Albert Camus. In other words, he was an eccentric, relentlessly interested in things for which others had little use.

I got to know him gradually, and we only really became friends once we'd left school. He briefly went up to Cambridge to study philosophy, but his illness got the better of him and he had to return home. This didn't matter much, of course. Jake was always an autodidact, better at teaching himself than being instructed. We'd go for coffee often when I was back on reading weeks.

One summer we travelled to France. The trip was a pilgrimage of a kind. We were trying to reach Lourmarin, a small commune about an hour from Marseille. We caught the Eurostar from London, and stopped off in Paris for a day or so. We spent the days hanging around cafes and bars near Saint-Germain, and in the evenings, we hung around bars. We chatted about politics and books. Jake used a Lime scooter to get about to save his lungs. I trailed behind, whistling the Marseillaise.

The second day we went to Montparnasse cemetery, to visit the occupants. The place radiates intellectual cachet. Or at least it would do, were it not crawling with American tourists. All of old Paris seem to be buried at Montparnasse, all slotted in between one another like pilchards in a tin. Samuel Beckett, Jean-Paul Sartre, Simone de Beauvoir, Emil Cioran. The expectation when visiting these places is to find something left of the dead, some trace of their essence still detectable on the air or the earth, like stale cigarette smoke. But Jake wanted to go to Montparnasse for a very specific reason—he wanted to see Raymond Aron's grave.

Old Ray took quite a while to locate, but eventually we found him, crammed in near the back wall of the cemetery. It was a tall, Hebrew-inscribed tomb. Previous visitors had left their trinkets and tchotchkes: pieces of glass, worn smooth by the sea. Foreign coins. And yet for all this, neither of us felt anything much. Aron was an intellectual, and now he lay in the ground. That was all the tomb meant.

Coffee, bookshops, alcohol—so the trip continued. Then the day arrived when we were to leave Paris and head south. In a cab on the way to the train station Jake had a coughing fit. The driver looked over his shoulder in alarm and asked: '*Tu malade?*' I did my best with GCSE French. '*Désolé—il avait mucoviscidose.*' The driver nodded, but opened all the windows anyway, fearful of whatever was inside Jake's embattled lungs.

So there we were, aboard the TGV, barrelling southward through rural France. We chatted most of the way. Jake is probably one of the most interesting people to talk to I know. He can quote, at length, endless anecdotes about a variety of philosophers, and reel off entertaining summaries of very obscure books. His sense of humour is unswervingly dry.

A NOTE ON THE AUTHOR

We stayed in a hotel by Saint Charles station, and had dinner in Marseille that evening. The city was not what I'd expected. The boulevard outside the station was littered with soiled mattresses, and the city as a whole seemed to me very badly run down. It didn't really matter to us, though. We didn't really care about Marseille.

The next morning, we got up at first light, and spent half an hour trying to read the bus timetable. There was only one bus per day that connected to Lourmarin, via Aix-en-Provence. Slowly, we came to understand that the bus was leaving from the depot behind the train station—in five minutes. We dashed round to the back of the station and boarded the bus just as it was about to leave. It took several hours to reach Aix-en-Provence, where we had to change busses. There was a further hour or so to wait until the bus to Lourmarin, so we sat in a deserted café and cracked jokes. A man walked past in sunglasses with a comically long baguette under his arm. Jake and I agreed that France—while populated mainly with ordinary French people—contains a fairly considerable population of 'stock_frenchman.jpg', which we agreed was reassuring.

By the time we got to Lourmarin, the crispness of the morning had softened into a clear Mediterranean afternoon. We got off the bus and watched it trundle up the hill, until the sound of its engine merged with the chorus of cicadas, and disappeared. Overhead, a plane traced a thin white line across the humid blue sky.

As luck would have it, the cemetery was just opposite the bus stop, on the outskirts of town. It put me in mind of a Roman ruin: the crumbling perimeter wall, the thin cypress trees that stood straight and still in the breezeless air. The grave didn't take so long to find this time. We walked around along the paths between the graves, white gravel crunching underfoot.

It was a simple grave, more modest than others in the cemetery. It being the height of summer, a blooming shrub flooded the grave with delicate red-pink flowers. I think it was a rhododendron, or maybe an oleander. Camus lay next to his wife, Francine Faure, in the solitude of a French valley.

As we stood there, surrounded by lush green hills of Provence, the prospect of death seemed suddenly less frightening. I can't quite explain why. It felt as though death didn't mean abject existential oblivion, but a period of peace, of returning to oneness with the natural world. A kind of oceanic feeling descended. Above all, it was the sense of an eternal summer.

We didn't talk much as we approached the village. A steep, narrow street led us between the ancient buildings, and we encountered no one. So silent was the village of Lourmarin that it might've been abandoned. Eventually we came to a small square with cafés and restaurants, where we sat down and had lunch. Americans, it seemed, had even reached areas of France so remote as Lourmarin. 'Oh yeah there's great wine in France' said one of them. 'The wine here's fucking great—get a load of this stuff!' Jake rolled his eyes, and gave a rare wry smile.

So that's Jake; as I know him, at least. Although the main subject of Jake's writing is the experience of illness, this selection of essays you are about to read covers various topics. It covers everything from Raymond Aron and liberalism, to the death of Jake's beloved cat, Lemons. This essay selection is therefore much like Jake himself: eclectic, and intellectually challenging.

—William Fear

Foreword

I'M CAUGHT between being an outspoken moralist, and what I perceive as more pragmatic political analysis. It is difficult for these modes to be congruent with each other, as it is easy to make correct moral statements that nonetheless won't cross the threshold into reality. Immediate moral statements, made passionately, might suppose, or wish, for opponents or enemies to just wise-up, or vanish, and it might be a just suggestion that they do so. But this is foolish in serious politics, as our opponents won't just disappear because we dislike them, or simply accept our arguments. Or statements might involve, from me, hyperbole and heightened emotions we can conceive as fair, given my pain, even if they amount to no change in technical policy. Sartre said to Aron that he was often too afraid to make a fool of himself. Aron conceded he was right in this criticism, as scientific progress can require making mistakes, chance, mistakes can even be profitable, and Sartre's lack of fear allowed him to be more creative. Yet in politics Sartre 'made generous use of his right to be wrong', so his creativity wasn't always so prudent. Too many aberrations make it difficult to justify loyalty, even to a great creative, so I would prefer on balance to be more boring and truthful than engaging and creative, even if creativity may often get the better of me.

The following essays, I think, show a mix between open creativity, moral pleas, moral bargaining, and at least attempts at more cogent analysis where my previous moralism might not be practical. Should I really be so afraid of being impractical? I've been praised for my truth, on expositions of my illness and feeling, and these can't be mutually exclusive with a dry analysis of realism and policy. If I'm wrong here, and I'm indeed fine to express harsh emotions freely, I'm equivocating only out of caution. I think my life with illness, and a generally rough experience, give me some leeway to be rude and emotional, and we should be able to accept my different moods and their contradictions.

The following articles include personal, memoirist venting, and something amounting to an assessment of various phenomenologies, political realities, or a history of ideas. If not true scholarship, which I won't attest to.

Most of the following articles and essays appeared in issues of the quarterly literary magazine *Exacting Clam*, while some are new pieces published here for the first time. For vain reasons I enjoy them being collated in an accessible collection, so I hope you may appreciate them too.

And thank you to Wend Rend for her wonderful illustrations.

—Jake Goldsmith

Contents

A Note on the Author, by William Fear — v

Foreword — ix

From Royal Papworth Hospital — 3

On CF and Possibility — 9

Disabled Thoughts — 15

Yet More Thoughts — 23

Specious Stuff — 41

Distrust and Expertise — 59

A Brief Note About Aronian Liberalism — 65

Worse Than a Crime — 79

Words and Clarity — 93

Lemons — 101

Illustrations

Panes and Pains	2
In Extremis	8
How to Have a Heart	10
Convenience	16
Inhospitable	22
Sight	39
Montaigne & Clementine	40
Loop	58
What Would Aron Do?	64
Is That All There Is?	80
Crosstalkers	92
Hint of Lemons	100
Last Blossom	107

IN HOSPITAL ENVIRONMENTS

From Royal Papworth Hospital

My condition has been very serious, the worst it has ever been.

I won't be coming out of hospital any or much healthier than when I came in, despite improvements. Which means I will need oxygen at home now. The general trend is downwards. Annoyingly, the doctors can be equivocal about it and you need to read between the subtle lines, because they're not Dutch about things.

I was very, very unwell, more than my parents or doctors realised, when I was admitted and they have been pretty worried about me. It was 50/50 at one point, quite honestly, and everyone was on edge.

I am improving on some level; I am eating and maybe gaining some weight. I am making small improvements with my oxygen saturation and so there are upwards trends. But the overall trend with my illness is down and they talk about me ominously. Frankly they're (at least some of them) bad at it—they're not good at either being clear and precise for fear of being too cutting, and they're too vague otherwise. They only sometimes like to be straightforward when it's right near the brink, I believe, when talking to CF patients about their prognosis. Unsure. Hard to say. Some are better than others.

I should be out of hospital, hopefully, in the next couple weeks. Despite my tone, I am actually improving every day and more capable of doing things, more and more each day. There is good news. But all optimism is tempered, I have a long way to go, and in the longer term cystic fibrosis still is what it is (a horrid phrase, but apt, surely).

When I'm out of hospital and no healthier than when I came in, but still a bit better, that means walking will be just as limited as it was. I'll need my wheelchair more and I'm likely going to struggle with basic things like stairs.

My friend Will proposed going for walks and being stern with me—that won't be possible. I will be able to walk a limited amount but will be dependent on the wheelchair.

I have also heard doctors speaking to Mum when I am half-asleep, or when they think I am asleep they talk to her. Again, they have been ominous and bleak in their tone, but in a calm way at least, if that somehow makes it less frightening.

Death reduces everything to indecision, as Larkin said. It paralyses you. I look at what's coming and I'm a rabbit in headlights. There's no escape, no reprieve. No better whined at than withstood. Bravery lets no one off the grave. I just have friends to comfort me before I'm hit. I have maybe a few years left, again it's hard to tell. It's all precarious.

I have zero spiritual comforts. All, always, seemed like alien nonsense. I don't like it, but I think it's hubris to assume we could know anything else behind or beyond the most basic observation. I guess I cope with what could be called a 'material sensualism of friendship'. Epicurus is basically backwards on every point except one: 'Of all the means which are procured by wisdom to ensure happiness throughout the whole of life, by far the most important is the acquisition of friends'.

Everything else is myth. I've written about it and thought about it enough already, it tires me. I just want to get out without much pain and bruising.

At least I have plenty of people to talk to, though; or I write to them.

There's always been a different phenomenological awareness around death for me because its fact is always neurotically present in my mind and it's harder to forget it than if I were not unwell. It's always been there. That awareness doesn't make it easier to face or less scary. In some ways I'd rather be taken out in an instant, unaware. Or in my sleep. I'm just glad and immensely grateful I have support.

There's always something I call 'pub talk', where hard and grizzled men, or really anyone, in the comfort of a pub or café with a drink and friends will idly talk about suicide or euthanasia. 'I'd rather you shoot me dead than let me slip away with dementia'; but 90% of the time this is all talk, where few, myself included, will really be prepared for the animal grief and agony, or even the boring listlessness, of death or coming upon death. Most won't know what to do, or remain paralysed, or don't think about it at all. Or don't get a choice at all—which may somehow be the better option.

'Achieving worldly wisdom in humility and self-awareness still does not prepare for the final experience, for real grief, by plan and prediction. Virtuous instructions don't prepare one, coolly, in experience for agony. You cannot inoculate yourself, or tranquillise yourself, outside of words with a supreme effectiveness. You're too impotent and your mind isn't the psychic inquisitor of the heart. It's a poor old man giving occasional advice and direction. It may not be followed, and maybe sometimes it shouldn't. I won't say definitely and I lack the intelligence'.

I find it much too difficult to account for my emotions consistently. I feel numb or aloof most of the time. It's only occasionally a shock—not a surprise, but a shock. It's often more creeping and looming than something acute. I think my most common emotion is feeling completely adrift.

It's popular to call this 'disassociation', but really when I see it described like that by people who appear, in my sanctimony, as normal and conventional people able to participate in society in everyday quotidian ways I cannot fathom, they're Holden Caulfields or Bojack Horsemans. Faux and fashionable 'depression for normies' that I'm perennially outside of—beyond.

If I express that in the wrong tone, I seem arrogant. Yet I've done enough self-loathing, I don't feel arrogant, and friends, at least, tell me that my experience should trump the perceptions of a blithe public. I have always been wary of appearing sanctimonious just by speaking bluntly, and I have to keep being assured by others that it is actually fine for me to think these things, and with less equivocation and self-policing.

I'm in a pessimistic mind where I don't expect any grand things from life and I value the mundane. I don't expect much at all in the sense of achieving real justice in the world—justice that is sustainable and lasting—and nor do I expect much in the path of avoiding ecological catastrophe. We're doomed and all we can do is mitigate damages and try not to hasten our annihilation.

But that's no excuse for putrid nihilism. I'll still want people to try to do good things because mitigating suffering, even without any grand ideals, is a good end in itself—and I am not one for augmenting injustice and suffering when injustice is so abundant. You could pithily call it optimism without hope.

I wish all my friends and closest family the best lives and the best futures, and they should still work for it, stalwart in the face of all cruelties. Those I love dearly and who have given me the sense of gratitude needed to live, I owe them my life. I hold their hands tightly.

May 2020

ON CF AND POSSIBILITY

SCIENCE-FICTION WRITERS have been known to default to using cystic fibrosis as an example of a disease that will simply be eradicated by gene modification. This is due to a wider perception of what the illness is, and also to popular perceptions of the advancement of genetics research, and our knowledge and control over genetics. This includes the optimistic, even transhuman ideas that feature the overcoming, through knowledge, of nature—and scientific, or technological, utopianism, in a broader sense. Even our fundamental reckoning with nature, with death, and of escaping it. Big things we are playing with here.

Cystic Fibrosis research has seen the development of a newer generation of drugs, such as Kaftrio and others, with a lot of hope and investment placed in them that they may essentially eradicate many, if not all, of the problems people with CF will face—this being a step towards further exciting research.

This is only partly true, and we have to be blunt here. It also represents in a greater sense a fundamentally misguided optimism about human control and capability, including the idea of the eventual eradication of all disease and disability.

To put it simply, this is hubris.

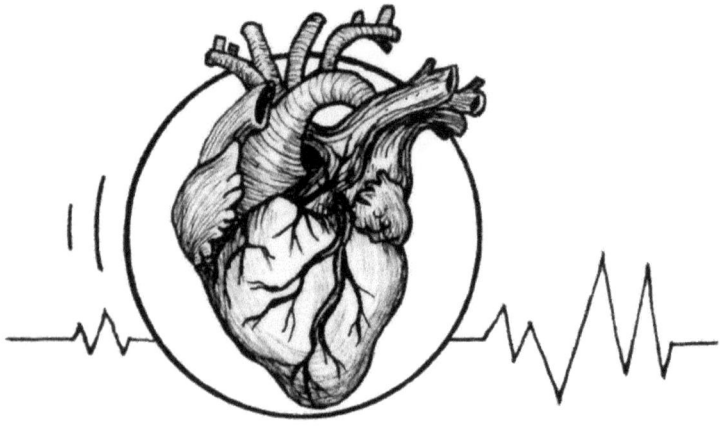

More specifically, these newer drugs have been and can be of some benefit to those with more common CF mutations, and you may well know people who have seen some great improvements. What is neglected are those for whom these drugs are not even an option to begin with due to the incompatibility of their mutations. CF can be caused by thousands of different mutations in millions of different permutations, some of them utterly unique. Again, more broadly, despite the temptation to believe otherwise, we do not understand as much about genetics as we think, and much of it remains nebulous. Neurology, psychiatry, genetics—these are all more complex fields of medicine than we admit. They will remain less understood by us than we would like, even with growing technological advancements, and they are definitely not well-conceived by hubristic quack and woo understandings of either the human body or of life generally.

You may point to the more optimistic stories and begrudge my pessimism, but here's the thing: you fucking always point to the optimistic stories. Less than glowing accounts frighten and discomfort you, so that you constantly remind us of good news and vague hopes. But you appear less concerned with my own discomfort and terror—a terror far more acute than your outside view because I'm the one who will actually face these choices, the pain, and all these contentions being thought about neurotically and every day. You aren't in my body. You go to work and interact with conventional society while I sit (most of the time) indoors with far less to distract me—barely coping with my bodily functions and thinking about my expiration date. Forgive me if tales of success and sugar-coating don't bring me joy. They're distant. I prefer my hard truth to your fretting over what's happening to me and what is possible for me. I'm the one experiencing this. You think *you're* uncomfortable or scared, seeing me as some grim example or an unsettling reminder of grave things, but I'm the one actually having to live this. I am consumed by righteous indignation—born, as I see it, into a cruel world that was immediately unjust to me, unjust in volumes to so many others, with no convincing metaphysical or cosmological justification for any of it at all, with only mundane things being of any possible comfort: friends and family offering some solace. I'd be animated and angry if I wasn't so absolutely drained of fortitude.

I'm happier and more good-humoured in other writing.

And no, you don't think about life and death like this—not habitually. Death may be real to you but it is also much more distant; it is faraway or accidental, you are young, and not many actually live life unto death, in a consistent sense at least. You can afford not to think about it given that it is far less pressing. God, I have written all this shit before! If you don't want to get it then you won't. It's a matter of your life and view on things being comprised of such different concerns. You aren't ill!

I wrote a whole fucking book about this with the perverse intention of it standing as a testament to who I am and what I believe—that could be read as an easy biographical introduction to me. It details a phenomenology of illness and a life defined through the lens of chronic illness. I took the title of the book (*Neither Weak Nor Obtuse*) from a phrase in a letter Boris Pasternak sent to Albert Camus, regarding sensualism as our only recourse in life—in that such may be the case, but if it is utterly naked (i.e. unfettered and extreme), and holds similar conceits to supernatural or theological salvation, then it becomes weak and obtuse. Struggling with this brand of materialism without the availability of convincing spiritual or metaphysical avenues is a major part of this phenomenology.

Returning to the fabled wonder drugs (as they're described): for those who are genetically eligible to take these newer drugs, they can come with numerous side effects and intolerances (sickness, mood swings, a long list of other complications) that may make their use impossible. Beyond 'miracle drugs', transplantation and other 'fixes' for the symptoms of CF are not so amazing either. Transplantation can only, commonly, offer a few more years if successful, if that, and otherwise comes with multiple recurrent risks such as organ rejection. Or it may just not work at all. And for all the healthy, non-disabled people out there who can idly and blithely say things, as you always do: the world is much more complicated than you think, and this is not your choice.

I want to be allowed to be angry. When I am stoical or childishly funny, remaining stern and academic or making jokes at everything and not taking much seriously, I am better tolerated. I use humour and have a playful sense of childishness. I don't think I'm very funny in my writing, because I only write about intimate things—which can of course be funny, but I mostly do so very seriously. I express love and adoration and gratitude. For once I want to be absolutely enraged and not feel regretful about it afterwards. I feel an ambivalence towards prolonging my life if it will be too painful. I value comfort more highly. I want quiet. The world is unjust and I hate it, yet I have little hope in correcting it. I just want to relax in the garden.

Whether people think they are fonder of scientific understanding or have stock in other hopes, a trend they share is a massive over-estimation of human possibility and progress, as well as a perception that disability and ill-health are fixable, or eventually fixable, phenomena we can comprehensively grapple and come to terms with. Bluntly, disability is much more complex than this. Illness is far more complicated and bemusing than you ever think it is. And while it is certain that we will see medical advancements, the reach and potential of these need to be more truthfully considered. For far too many these presumed hopes are remote, or simply ableist nonsense. Enthused, toxic optimism from non-disabled voices about 'cures' and fixes (especially considering many different disabilities or health concerns) is insulting, or even flagrant eugenicist evil. Cystic Fibrosis is a far different question from Deafness, or Down syndrome—

obviously. If I expand on that more I may as well write volumes, so I will leave that to others. It's not in my current scope to talk about all the variances and politics of disability, despite my wide digressions here. There are far more political barriers to disability justice than are considered, and frankly most have no idea, much of the time, about these different dimensions and what lives people live: with what they have to face each day and contend with so regularly.

There is a constant condescension and a stock ignorance regarding ill health. Even a global pandemic hasn't stopped people living as callously as they want, and the whole history of life-changing pandemics (this was never unprecedented) that have caused such massive change throughout all of history—more so than any war or political upset—remains ubiquitously ignored or unknown. It's unsurprising that hubris and ignorance remain so established.

So yes, I have been doing okay recently.

May 2021

Disabled Thoughts

I ONLY EVER make long posts to my friends on social media that aren't just silly pictures when I'm unhappy and in a bad place. Every time I am (yet again) in hospital I am depressed, but I am safer (I think) in my hospital room.

I am in hospital this time (January 2022) partly because it is unsafe to be outside or even at home. My family have to work, my mum works in a school and schools are a primary vector for transmitting disease. Many healthcare workers are likely to be infected at home once close to their children.

My sister works in hospitality, catering to callous and uncaring people behaving recklessly as they eat and drink and party.

One of the hardest things about the pandemic as a vulnerable person has been watching people I know and care about do reckless shit that more or less communicates that they don't really care what my quality of life is.

My family try to keep me safe, but they can't control the actions of the wider public who may still infect them, as if it is somehow their choice to infect someone with a preventable, deadly disease. It is not one's free choice to murder others.

And then the news of what the U.K. wishes to do on its so-called 'Freedom Day' (July 2022) is truly murderous. Se-

rial killers are condemned for directly murdering people, but implementing policies that kill thousands somehow doesn't receive equal reproach. Twelve years of austerity and the slow neglect and killing of disabled people was bad; this casual eugenics just continues.

It's exhausting how many people are of the mind that: "I'm not a eugenicist, how dare you call me that, but also I do believe my convenience is more important than our collective safety and the weak and inconvenient should simply vanish from society." The pandemic being over means actually doing things to mitigate the spread of the virus and protect people from infection and death. So many believe in lies (about virology or life generally) at the expense of those most at risk. Other nations are better at this. Not doing stuff, not making sacrifices because you are weak-willed and privileged, means it will continue. Unrestricted behaviour without limitations means more death and an unfree, further inaccessible society.

Most do not care about those who haven't been able to go out and live due to the risk increased with their disability, or those who still have to but aren't given proper accommodations and support. The gall of some to say we have been successful in saving lives is a gross lie; the U.K. especially has done abysmally through this whole period.

People's words and petty defences mean less than their actions, which have only perpetuated harm towards people they revile or just do not care about.

Many disabled people and those who would still effectively be shielding are abandoned as the rest of society prefers the nasty, brutish, and short life to actually having our short time be worth anything.

I am already close to death and don't wish to be closer due to the callousness of others. Even before the pandemic my life was isolated and lonely, mostly depressed and ruminating on my shortcomings and my impending death. What's my projection? I've long maintained that it will be miraculous for me to reach 30 years old. I nearly died in May (2021). Any attempt I have to be happier or more optimistic feels like lying to myself. And each day I feel like I have less and less of an opportunity to do things. What could be considered worse in various ways than being explicit, obvious Nazis is that essentially millions of people across the world view mandates and their "personal freedoms" (when they are already free to do whatever the Hell they want, with no real idea of what lacking freedom actually means) as more important than life and death for vulnerable people. Do I have to temper my condemnation? Spurious ideas about "the economy" or one's own convenience and choice to be harmful matter more than death, for them. They may recoil at the most obvious fascist tendencies or violent actions yet they are fine to actively contribute to or ignore death, suffering, and the real lack of freedoms. Mass death via neglect, incompetence, and indifference to life is as savage as death by malice and intent. Statistically it amounts to the same weight in corpses. The former is less expensive too, so people can remain comfortable while it happens and convince themselves that they are actually on the side of liberty and justice while depriving us of those very things—at least the so-called explicit Nazis or eugenicists are honest and you know where they stand. At least stab me in the front.

Am I too radical? Am I too hyperbolic? Am I exaggerating? Is it all too much? I know I am so wonderfully morally superior but am I upsetting them? I'm not even a terrorist or a killer and I don't implement or support polices that kill thousands of the most vulnerable people alive, but I guess I'm the bad one.

Disability and illness, and what they represent in all their variances, have an existential weight attached to them. They are then often deliberately overlooked, undervalued, with their representations preferred dead or out of the way. One of the most fundamental aspects of existence is viewed instead as a narrow lens, a niche, rendered as unimportant or as malignant—out of fear, shame, utilitarian malevolence or stock ignorance. Misunderstood and put at a distance. Disability and its implications are reviled as they're not a comfortable presence for many people.

Popular culture in any nation will not contend with pain, grief, illness, or disability (not always synonymous, but still) in any truly commendable or genuine way. We simply do not cope with life. Disability or ill-health is viewed as a personal failure to not work or do better before it is comprehended simply as reality often inescapable reality. And the needs of disabled people will always come after the needs of those who aren't so when it most matters. Casual eugenics is the preferred state of affairs for many of us before accepting disabled life. Whole industries, much of civilisation, even, is dependent on making illness an easily comprehensible personal fault and truly escapable through enough effort, money, or spirit. Values held so commonly deem life worthless if it cannot be 'productive' in what is ultimately a terrible way to spend our short time.

Heaven forbid you make the healthies uncomfortable. One better not present a less than heroic image, lacking any glitzy optimism, no hard grit, or show anything that may make them a little upset. If illness is not presented in a way that makes those who aren't ill or disabled comfortable, in their aloof world removed from real concerns, then good luck. Allow me to be a bit miserable. Or if I am somehow jovial, I don't need false hope.

Pain and its minimisation, being able to be merely comfortable with the tiniest reprieve, is more important to me than most else. I am too ambivalent towards continuing life if doing so means being in an amount of pain than makes prolonging not worth the cost. This doesn't then mean drugging me into complete catatonia so I feel nothing, I simply want to live without being so exhausted, without so much stress, before my premature death that I absolutely terrified of. I don't want to shorten my life, but I end up being complacent and unable to do things that would prolong it because they cause far too much discomfort and distress.

The callous then suggest that not being able to stoically handle such pain is weakness or a moral failing. I will reserve using the worst words that I have for them.

I repeat that these people live in an entirely different and dismissive universe unattended to some of the most vital rudiments of the human condition—which involve sickness and disability. They believe the conceit that rendering life through the lens of disability is reductive, rather than experiencing life with a more essential primary theme. Obviously this does not mean that sick or disabled people are now soothsayers or immediately more knowing of the truth, and I hold no room at all for fetishisation or self-flagellating glorification, but, rather . . .

> . . . this matter of ill-health is more personal, more essentially of the ego than anything in the world; more than love, for that can be given expression; more than

religion, because that is a satisfaction in itself; more than fear, for that passes. Pain is personal, before everything. Only one who has experienced it in some measure can understand its significance in life.

[Richmond H. Hellyar in *W. N. P. Barbellion* (1926)]

I just want some respite, even if true peace is impossible. Just treat people a little better.

January 2022

Yet More Thoughts

I HAVE SOME TROUBLE with writing. I want to write more, write a wider cultural history of things I know about (disability/illness, eugenics, dead intellectuals), but everything I write is navel-gazing. I don't like impersonal writing, I'm not adept at it and nor do I want to be. I much prefer memoir and diary as a more direct engagement with ideas, though I can't help but feel anything I write about the pandemic or whatever else is yet more morose navel-gazing, more of me complaining about insoluble problems while pontificating on the fact that I'm very sad and ill. It can tire a reader, and why should they care?

There's a place for this indulgence and I will defend it when it's unfairly chastised by snobs, but there's surely more I can do than repeat the same talk about my own feelings and failings. Or at least I'd want to do this in a way that doesn't feel like I'm retreading the same territory over and over again.

I wrote my memoir (*Neither Weak Nor Obtuse*) in an insular way so it could hint at what my broader ideas are without having to expand so much, given I'm lazy. I don't need to write loads about Czeław Miłosz, for example. I can just say he's an influence.

I might want to write something in an interview format, or a dialogue between me and friends, or travel writing—

but travel is still difficult given the realities of my health and the pandemic. I'd hop over to Paris again, visit Raymond Aron's grave (again), stop by a few famous cafés and places I've researched. But I'm too anxious to do that any time soon, and it presents a material risk. I could otherwise write about my experience with The Barbellion Prize and accessing literary and publishing culture, but I'd prefer prompting from others to having to drag it up myself.

Unfortunately, most of my writing happens *in extremis*, which is to say, I'm only really motivated to write anything when I'm very ill, in hospital, etc., and I don't recommend this for the sake of art or anything else. I'd much prefer to have zero creativity and a less acrimonious life than go through a lot of pain and nonsense just to write a book or create something: I abjure the 'suffering artist'.

I'm far too judgmental about my writing. I upset myself when I look back at any previous writing and think how I could have simplified it or made it less verbose or made it less abstract and more straightforward. I don't want to write too plainly or boringly, and I try to make my writing organic and easy, but it still has a pompous quality, or it's littered with mistakes. It's odd that people will excuse prolixity from some authors and have their own nebulous, fashionable tastes about style, and it's hard to navigate this if you're insecure. I get some good reviews of my work, but it doesn't help much. I'm sure concerns like this are common but I'm too solipsistic and indulgent to gauge the mood of other writers. And it matters less what they think. I myself need to feel okay with my life and work—not for the sake of any explicit progress or advancement, but just so I can have some small sense of comfort instead of self-hatred.

I ask, why don't I like myself? It's not for any lack of positive affirmation, or others' exacting standards, or ever being told I'm not good enough. The opposite of that happens. I am always reassured of my own goodness, and I have care and support. I don't feel bad because I'm not succeeding greatly at grand things because I don't want grand things, like a career or status. I want a modest and quiet life and the avoidance of more pain and hassle. My ultimate dream is a quiet Hobbiton *cottagecore* life. I've always held my own work and behaviour to a higher standard and I rarely meet it. I saw somewhere recently that self-hatred was a form of narcissism, which I found perverse. As if I can't be satisfied by my efforts because I should be so much better, as if I could be that? The idea only makes me feel *more* useless. I'm now a narcissist because I'm dissatisfied with my life? I should be satisfied? Screw off.

I know otherwise that peace is pretty difficult in life, in politics, or anywhere. I don't even want to create something amazing, just something I can be okay with—attesting my existence to me, so I'm not so alone.

Most of what I write becomes repetitive, and I repeatedly face the question of why anyone should write at all when most of what could be said has already been said, and better than I could express. I think it'd be justifiable if I quit altogether. I don't have much of a good argument for others if they ask me why they should write besides, again, solipsism and emotional ventilation. I find myself and my writing embarrassing and no amount of talk or trying not to care changes this. I need regular praise, like a dog, or I feel sad and useless. How selfish of me.

※

There's too much information in the world. Worry about the over-abundance of new information and data is decades old by now; it only gets more cumbersome each day. The copiousness of information, so much of it extraneous and distracting, is trouble enough—in addition there is the social pressure to consume media and know so much about new events, where it can feel impossible to retreat and relax if one wants to remain at all conscious of truly important developments and have any say. If one doesn't care to have a say, then fine. Plenty say a lot with no care at all for being credible or responsible, and that has always been the case. This is bad enough, and then for even more worry and weariness we have the shaming and extortion of others for failing to keep up to date with absolutely everything, every new development in *the discourse*, every new trend, compounded and aggravated by the development of the technological society (oooh look, he referenced Ellul, isn't he clever . . .)—with its increased pace and new demands. It's possible, if spurious, to think it used to be easier, though perhaps less unforgiving, to not know of things, when there was still this extant pressure to be an engaged participant but not so exaggerated by the technological innovation of culture. Not that a reactionary antithesis to this would be much help, or even possible. Worse, people talk as if they really did know everything, with a tone and confidence suggesting so, when with so much more information existing now it's surely the case that proportionally they know even less of all there is to know. It's okay to not know things, to not be privy to everything, and one shouldn't face so much ire for not consuming such a huge quantity of media and information, especially when it's trivial or optional.

Abundance becomes a problem, argumentation online is difficult unless it is heavily curated or moderated; 'debate culture' is overrated, a rhetorical exercise, not a proper *pedagogy*—or in less fancy words, it's not the way one learns and reflects best on ideas. There are too many voices shouting over each other, many with insincere or glib motivations—many more that are plainly uninformed, many others violent—for most to glean any real knowledge or wisdom, and it becomes more difficult to find what is genuinely insightful when it's subsumed by so much vitriol and noise. Unless you're wanting to know the nature of noise! It is better to limit oneself and engage in a broad overview of ideas at some distance, preferably guided by a wiser curation, while not immersed and lost in the mess of the crowd. I don't mean that one should retreat to absolute quietude or never challenge one's conceptions. Indeed, instead, you can always rethink things and interrogate yourself and your ideas and the wider world, and doing this does not require a full immersion into undiplomatic and abusive discourse which can instead be observed at a safe distance. One doesn't need to *talk* online with extremists to know them. I have become adept at observing the worst people, silently lurking in their spaces, a ghost they'll never see collecting a record of their follies.

It is possible to read and comprehend opposing ideas without getting involved in a venomous argument with an uncharitable interlocutor. Sometimes it is required, for the sake of safety and avoiding abuse. This idea is forgotten in online spaces, where the pressure to be *engaged* is so encouraged, regardless of any tact or responsibility, regardless of whether you know anything or not, and disengagement is considered rude or cowardly instead of healthy or respectful of one's limited resources.

Most arguments aren't sober: one is derailed and consumed by passion and emotion that is hard to direct usefully or efficiently. The faraway observation of foreign arguments can be more beneficial than being involved, just as a mountain can be better perceived for its true magnitude from afar, rather than with one's face in the dirt. I won't discount the possible utility of being closely involved in slanderous debate, and I'll even insist that regional and local knowledge, intimately involved, is vital for any bigger picture to ring true—but I'll contend that fully formed and cogent ideas are made best at a safer distance with the time and ability to reflect and review. At least for me, and at least if one doesn't have the time.

"Are most of our readings of theory not shoddy, as we pin down labels and allegiances? We name what we do not understand."

In June 2021, President Emmanuel Macron was slapped by a member of the public, a medieval combat enthusiast. Views varied on whether it was a deliberate, premeditated act of violence or an act of impulse. Investigating the background and the politics of the attacker, Damien Tarel, his beliefs were described as 'ideological mush'. This is easy to say when it's obvious, when someone's views are a hodgepodge of different influences and motivating violence. My reaction was almost snobbish. Most people are 'ideological mush'. Who isn't? It's funny when people think they aren't mushy.

People attest to or try to conceptualise others as having, somehow, a more or less consistent set of beliefs, especially when they are powerful, when a great majority of people are instead caught well within 'the muddledness of thought', or an otherwise vague sets of ideas, good, bad, everything in between, understood well or not, that are cobbled together as if they're impulsive consumers picking curious items from the store aisle. Consistent beliefs that could be easily described as monolithic, or non-hypocritical political or philosophical ideas are rare, or primitive and terroristic. In part, one wants some sort of diverse mixture of ideas—but the contention is how well-rounded and well-understood any regularly employed concepts and vocabulary are.

Popular pundits, filling the space of more humble intellectuals, more adept at carousing, looking attractive, better bullshitters, and better at advertising their wares, only have vague understandings of a variety of things they mush together. Some of those understandings are more lucid than others, while some are completely erroneous. William James warned of a professionalisation of academic and scholarly discipline that would distance truly learned thinkers from public spaces or make them less adept in public spaces than con-men, grifters, sophists, and others more capable, more hubristic, and less cautious than responsible authors. The arrogance of some professional academics, scoffing at the idea of public engagement or activism, further distances them from the public and laypeople—who then have their curiosities satiated by others far less responsible or knowledgeable. Forever a pessimist, I'd say James' warnings weren't heeded.

Few people have a real idea of how to properly define concepts and allegiances, misusing and misunderstanding all the usual and most common political vocabulary, all loaded with obnoxious connotations; some of them will have beliefs that are better constructed or more of a social conscience than others, but most are never going to be *that* thought out, and for anyone who does want some level of deeper and broader thinking or reflection, what they have most availably at hand is the great variety of modern punditry and not very many who are serious thinkers.

This doesn't mean I'm admonishing completely, or being sanctimonious, and saying everyone is stupid. Smarter people better understand ideas and events and will still be limited by preconceptions and experiences, or the narrowness of their expertise, and we lie if we say we are truly, and so often, coherent and acute in our understanding.

Believing in a sense of ideological consistency, or consistency of ideas that aren't so much ideological, becomes dubious when very average people, or even most people,

YET MORE THOUGHTS

will, say, hold beliefs reaching in all sorts of directions; where on one hand they can be pro-choice and against abortion restrictions, but also equally believe that all of #MeToo was a nefarious plot to discredit one's favourite actor.

Here's another subject that's been done to death, but I'll state it for the record regardless: given how technology and media have changed culture, if I'm being crude, the terms *public* and *intellectual* are often far apart. What's more common are people who are very public: pundits, clickbait YouTube video essayists, think tanks, networking accounts, newspaper columnists, who to some degree may be smarter than others (and may hold something valuable) but are often very much not serious theorists (though many will somehow think they are). Serious intellectuals still definitely exist outside the ivory tower, and definitely should, but many are restricted, professionalised, and do not have the same proportional public reach as past figures during the 19th and 20th centuries, where a different relationship between media, technology, and culture meant they could be afforded a different stage. There is no direct analogue in the 21st century, someone of the same level of both fame and expertise, to Jean-Paul Sartre or Andre Malraux, or Isaiah Berlin, in the public space—regardless of how right or wrong they were on things. Public intellectuals today are, in simplistic terms, afforded less fame and celebrity than in previous decades; and that public space is instead filled by those with less ability or creativity.

This doesn't suggest the past was any better, but rather that people of the same intellectual weight and also the same public weight, with both real knowledge *and* fame, had an easier time existing in the past; whereas now, crudely, fame is easy but real knowledge is not. I won't be rude as there certainly are some YouTubers with intellectual weight—it'd be wrong to be so derogatory or elitist—and authors, teachers, etc. can still maintain something of a public presence, but the process of culture and technology has done more to proliferate terribly noisy pundits and sophists, less so anyone with real brains. It is easier to find 'science explainers' or people with deep, yet narrow expertise explaining to a common audience difficult scientific concepts as pop intellectuals, but philosophers, historians, sociologists, etc., with real quality are drowned out by noisy punditry in a way they weren't, at least so easily, in the past—with all the past's many faults—due to the internet, the easier availability for anyone to say anything publicly, and due to media democratisation.

I could argue, against what I've just said, that extremism, fascism, and genocide still occurred during an idealised age of *men of letters*, and the expansion of right-wing fanaticism and anti-democratic tendencies is extant whether it's in the mess of today's media or the limited media of the past. So what's the use of nostalgically yearning for better public intellectuals? As a pessimist, again, I'll complain and say maybe it's more difficult now given the quantity of voices. If we were alienated in the past, how about now?

In more basic terms, if you ask an average person to name a public intellectual today, they will name someone public, but not someone intellectual. If you asked someone this question before the 1990s, chances are they'd more easily name someone with both qualities.

People who are 'real intellectuals' who are also known public personas still exist. Charles Taylor in Canada (though he's about 91 now), John Gray in the U.K., professors like Timothy Snyder, who has both an imagination and a social conscience (which can be rare), and acts partly as an activist and also a serious intellect with real credentials and quality.

There are otherwise 'intellectual entertainers' who will have a good thing to say or possess some real brilliance, in some capacity, but are still closer to 'populist intellects' rather than critical scholars.

Who am I to say all this? I'm just a small boy and a fool and I'm certainly not very well qualified. I don't have a serious academic understanding of many, many things. I'm far closer to tedious and noisy talking-heads than I am to serious scholarship.

I don't mean to be so sanctimonious. Those with a lack of expertise can still reflect and parrot what's been said by greater minds, and someone lacking rigour and real schooling can still say stuff that is essentially just and correct—and sometimes more so, with more of a social awareness and moral consciousness than cloistered academics. Being smart doesn't always mean having good judgement.

The wish, sent out into the world with little hope of any change, is for more humble, responsible, and insightful people to have an improved standing in public affairs. I've said before, grimly, that we get the intellectuals and celebrities we deserve. If they aren't very good or very smart, that might reflect on us. I'd hope we could do better.

Part of me wants to forget the unforgettable. Unlike many (at least evidenced by their behaviour), I can't be blithe and forgetful about the pandemic, minimise its impact, equivocate on its wider implications or deny inconvenient truths, as I'd do so at a greater risk than others. Still, the cost of any greater awareness I have of painful realities and unfortunate events, the result of any 'doom-scrolling' as it is colloquially known, even of accounts I'd know to be cogent and devoid of any tabloid sensationalism, is emotional destitution and depression. I have to retreat from bad news and can't be some active force, as it ruins me emotionally, physically; it wrecks me and leaves me unable to do anything while I remain the whole time, anyway, most of the time, in my own home away from the world. I have to retreat and manage risks and the primary way I do this is simply by staying at home, not going out, even if others wished I might be less worried about everything—or if everything outside was less worrisome.

I can complain and moralise as much as I want; I could, if I really had the heart for it, reprimand anyone close to me who has anything to do with me for causal and passive, everyday behaviour that could possibly open me to harm, like a stingy, pedantic moralist condemning everyone for their unconscious contributions to harm. *No ethical consumption, no ethical reciprocity.* But I'm not well-disposed to destroying all my relationships by calling every person I know a eugenicist for their milder infractions: which is also not a helpful way of changing behaviour. And I'd sound a bit silly. It's not effective.

There's little I can do unless others improve their behaviour, or improve their policy. I'm too tired and ineffectual to be some sort of activist or moraliser, and I don't have any political influence to change laws or culture. How we historically dealt with cholera and legionella is by improving infrastructure and by public effort. Instead, with Covid, we indulge in the lie of personal choice—which means the choices of a majority to ruin other lives considered less important. There could be improvements to infrastructure: with ventilation, air purifiers, and more that could mitigate Covid—just as we have long-standing public health protections against the aforementioned cholera and other diseases. One occasionally sees quiet implementations of this infrastructure, though normally reserved for the rich—while anyone else is free to harm or appears to care less. People are more willing to protect against venereal diseases, less so respiratory ones—even if respiratory diseases spread more easily. The politicisation of basic health measures, its own contentious and storied affair one could devote volumes to, means this appears like a lost fight. Especially if one doesn't have the stamina to keep up.

Unfortunately, it is the greater will of the public to passively and easily get on with their lives and not make sacrifices or investments to protect others (and protect disabled people, especially). For them, it is easier to peaceably carry on with everyday activities and not change. If the cost of this action, or inaction, is mass disablement (and much more), they don't appear to care very much or it doesn't cross their minds. People find any reason to justify their lack of care, or they just ignore things. The risks of the pandemic are minimised, equivocated, rationalised, denied, or ignored before being faced with what real implications they bring. It means I and others like me have to be vigilant and make our own sacrifices, while others don't care if we die or if we are all infected with a particularly pernicious, yet preventable contagion over and over again. They might say they care, but they won't act. And all I'm doing here is venting.

Camus had a quote: "Stupidity has a knack of getting its way." It is easier to be stupid. It takes less thought and time, you don't have to be so careful, you can afford to be forgetful, and life doesn't seem as hard if you are stupid. Stupid ideas and stupid actions will proliferate and spread more easily than better ideas. Or, if we are more charitable: it's easier to be ignorant and get on with life in peace, along the path of least resistance, than do something mildly inconvenient.

It might be easier to incentivise behaviour with policy, as moralising won't work, but there's little sign of policymakers doing that unless nihilistic financiers become more explicitly concerned with the loss of working human capital to increasing disability. Others will deny life to the grave.

Eugenics, from its tamer and indifferent iterations up to its most explicit and actively violent variants, is present through the perceived left, centre, and right of many politics. Real concern for disabled lives is harder to find than we'd wish or otherwise commonly believe. Others think their political or philosophical adherences mean that of course they're on the correct side of history and morality, advocating for the needs of the oppressed—yet they're often inconsistent, myopic, and engage in the above behaviour anyway, and more dishonestly. If one thinks one's truths are *obviously true*, axiomatically true, historically inevitable, rather than true and with robust defence, it's typical to encounter dishonesty and endless rationalisations of falsehoods. Encountering an honest racist or an honest eugenicist is almost a relief insofar that one knows exactly where they stand, while others keep pretending they're virtuous or somehow sincerely believe in their good fight while they dismiss, deny, or fail to consider disability—and much else.

I don't want to harbour some aggrieved victim complex, but can I help that? It's still true, given the evidence and regular reminders, that disability and ill health, through most cultures, is regarded as revolting, disgusting, a morbid existential reminder, or otherwise undervalued when juxtaposed with healthier lives. I don't want to be so preoccupied with this anymore, but it's inescapable and I don't have much optimism about altering it. My life is risk mitigation, not progress.

I have to retreat and hope I'm lucky enough to escape things.

The quotidian revulsion, disgust, or mockery of disability hasn't reformed much since FDR had to make such a logistical effort to hide his disability from public view. There are legal progressions, representational progressions, and maybe in some spheres a moral progression where at least some now don't view sickness and disability as sinful and immoral. Stating this to non-disabled people, of many persuasions, often motivates them to feebly grasp at an idea of better principles: that we truly have progressed, that things are better . . . It takes very little evidence to disabuse one of this optimism, with even minor research into medical neglect, public humiliations, pervasive and common attitudes, and legal dead-ends. Both medicalised and socialised views on disabled life are not so morally improved. The 'optics' of disability, the consideration of how it will appear to casual observers, are still almost entirely negative or pitiable.

Donald Trump, one to always project a vain image, was only persuaded to receive real Covid treatment, once he tested positive, after being informed that if he waited too long he'd no longer be able to walk to his car or helicopter, but would need to use a wheelchair—which would look pathetic and weak. We couldn't have that.

Disabled people often feel a sense of political and social homelessness. They aren't accepted in reactionary communities with more overt ideas of a 'might is right' social order; it's difficult to find acceptance in many more progressive communities, whether they're perceptibly centrist, liberal, of the left, or anywhere else, as somehow disability is a subject where even the smartest of people remain grossly ignorant. It's hardly the fundamental philosophies and ideologies, which will be bad enough, but the blithe and causal, passive and everyday actions—the easygoing dismissal where it wouldn't even cross one's mind to consider this dimension. Activists hope, some sincerely and earnestly, others in desperation, that things may become better. In marketing these concerns, appearing far too morose and defeated isn't effective. But we don't have to go far to recognise a great sense of hopeless resignation to a world that will never accept us, where the animal fear of sickness and death reflects a wider, implicit refusal to

YET MORE THOUGHTS

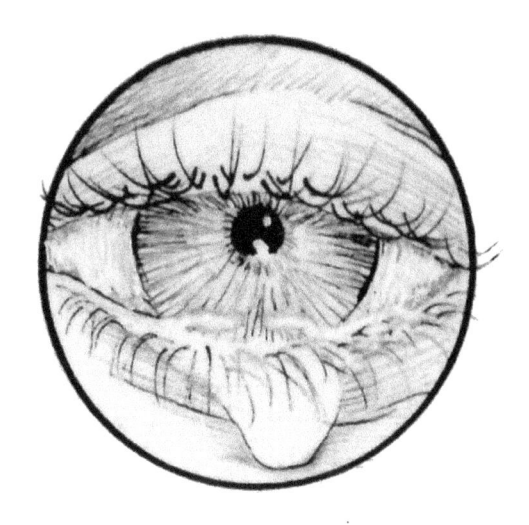

ever consider us equal persons, in each utilitarian scenario or appeal to deontological worth.

I don't want to appear heroic, or saintly, and I am always wary of receding into a traumatised victimhood offering no escape or respite. Self-flagellation isn't helpful, and aggressive indignation fails to persuade many of anything but further alienation and hostility. I am endlessly critical of both poles of righteous activism and polite society for ineffectively coping with structural issues, or ideological, teleological, pedagogical or personal issues. I don't want to be hopeless while surrounded by everyone's failure.

My only attempt is an intimate appeal, to those I know, to those whom I have some currency with, to make some small effort towards a world that isn't so cruel.

March 2023

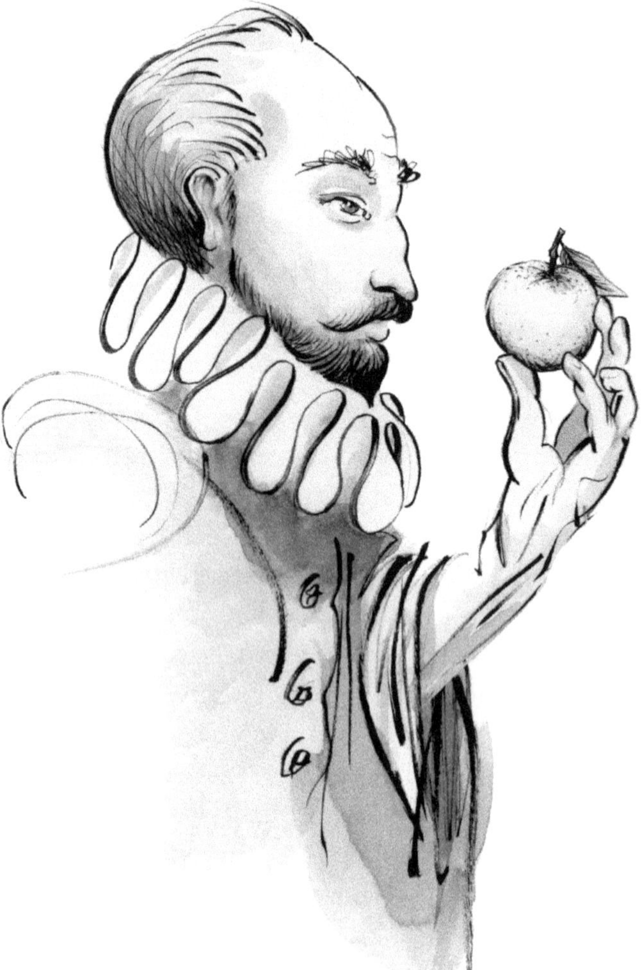

SPECIOUS STUFF

When I write I don't lie, and I find that perverse. There's something one could describe as a noble effort to write for uncommercial reasons, but I write for reasons I find difficult, nebulous, and yet crude or vulgar—somehow. There is no noble purpose, no higher purpose, no wish to inspire others or improve the world—as I have no confidence that I could do that.

Do I write the same thing each time? Surely. Thomas Bernhard essentially wrote the same book every time but pulled it off. I don't want to harp on one note of morose concern, but if I have (yet again) no higher purpose and writing is a ventilation system, then fine. I know my limits, nor can I write some comprehensive cultural history or an academic treatise that would satisfy review and scrutiny, nor do I have much inclination or ability to write fiction. I'll stick to confessionals and memoir. I might coin a useful turn of phrase and please a critic or a friend.

I'm told I've changed someone's life. Or several lives. My own small opinion prevents accessing my mind enough for it to change my emotions. I don't need to go over why I have a small opinion. I write with a conscious effort to be indulgent, and it matters less to me if this alters anyone's view or makes something outside twitch. It's all for me, I deserve to have less pressure, fewer solemn and overburdened senses interrupting my desired quiet. Yet I'm told it's worth something.

If I have previously written something like an epitaph, the last polemic of an expiring person, one questions what else I might still do. I reflect Barbellion's problem, where his writing was published but had, as part of its purpose and composition, the quality of being a last word. He would live a little while longer, and in a strict sense there was some lying about his death in that it didn't come *as* suddenly; yet in a fairer sense it was no lie, as the truth of his worries and reflections remained and the idea that a chronology off by a little would render it wrong is unjust. Even if I have in mind the morbid idea that I'm writing as if I am to expire the next day, the embodied prescience concerning what I'm going to experience, and surely when that present approaches my prediction of woe is nearly flawless, I still want life. I am grim but this does not delete goodness from my existence. Clearly the opposite happens, I must treasure little intimacies and not see forgettable touches as mundane. I eke out to live and say more against nothing. When I'm slowed down to indecision the insurmountable fear doesn't have a full grip. Comfort is partial, so fear is partial, friendship is partial. A truce is made where survival may become less daunting, and if more is available to me I can accept it graciously.

◌ Lazy, Anti-Intellectual Fruit Enjoyer

Most media I consume, as we are always consuming media, is passive and simple. I don't need depressive expositions that I'm well adept at already, and I don't spend all my time reading Montesquieu or Marc Bloch. Arrogantly, I've done enough and have little to prove to myself. I like these characters, as they are sometimes closer to characters, for me, and occasionally I'll take more than a dip and seep in a full immersion; but I watch YouTube gaming videos for crude banter and throwaway foolishness before taking in most else. It's much easier and I gain more from it immediately.

I don't like poetry. Over ninety-nine percent of it. Sometimes it might make me stop as I confront some depth, but most is shit or pretentious—in the strict definition of seeing more to something than what's actually there. I'm not moved by most art—it's images. I rarely feel more than mild interest. Very anti-intellectual of me. An inadequacy. But I feel things very intensely, I'm always intense about something, I certainly abhor anti-intellectualism. It's all very yucky and I mock those who decry it or are too dim to value or know basic information, or knowledge.

I remember a story of an older student who brought a collection of oranges and clementines into his university seminar and ate them messily. He wasn't careless or littering, but was at least clearly noticeable. When he was asked what he was doing and then to stop, he bluntly replied, "I like fruit—I can't eat metaphysics."

I found this hilarious and agreeable. If I was more confident I'd perform the stunt myself, but I've always said I'm a weasel and again I can't discount scholarship even if I am not the one to do it, or if it bores me, or doesn't contribute to my survival. At least that's the mature answer to give, because metaphysics does matter, yes . . . I'd rather eat an orange in my quiet home before reading Croce again. A younger me would scream at this indolence, and it's rude to deny some brilliance, but I guess I have more important, expedient needs than Italian philosophy—and have for some time.

Things are true simultaneously. Great art and scholarship exist; it's just not always for me.

Here's my flippant personal hack to achieve the appearance of being smart:

Raymond Aron was prescient about things and better read than most contemporaries. Kołakowski was generally correct about Marxism and Communism, Unamuno with the *Ethic of Doubt* has a decent ontology as ontologies go. Most only know Camus as a caricature and he suffers from the same fate as many over-famous writers, which is to say, being known only superficially. But he's not too complex, really; and Montaigne did a lot of things very broadly before they were cool. Fanon is right (about grievances) and wrong (about solutions) simultaneously: his violence is rather optimistic. Avoid modern clichés and euphemisms to look more sane and less ridiculous (unless it's just a bit), and be born with a life-limiting chronic illness to give you an air of mystery, humility, intriguing desperation, and a great excuse to get out of work and be vulgar. You deserve it!

☾ Fear and Happiness

I've long lost track of exactly how many times I've been in hospital. I neglect saying much about it because most days merge into incoherence anyway and I lose track. I don't enjoy being incredibly public about my health, but being silent feels like a capitulation, and I don't tolerate the loneliness. Ill health is a very lonely experience and my most prominent feeling since I can remember coherently has been loneliness (in and with my health) and aloofness from others because of it. I like to be silly, juvenile, and mischievous as a wily defence—an escape from a more pressing reality that's mean and painful.

Something I wrote in my memoir: "Relatives and friends may read too much into my pain. They might try to help me too much. I don't want to be suffocated with sympathy. At the same time, I deserve some level of sympathy and recognition for what is actually going on with me. It would be one thing if people could take one look at me and understand everything there is to know (i.e. all the relevant information and history which explains my current condition), but that is not the case. People don't know unless I bring it to their attention. This can serve to generate even more confusion if I fail to convey things properly. So then there is the wish to not say anything at all. But staying completely silent, while perhaps preventing me from ever being wrong about anything, almost guarantees that no one will notice the pain I endure. This problem extrapolated into wider concerns certainly gives us some doubt and fear."

I often prefer some level of silence and not revealing everything that's going on, as is my right, because what I feel is embarrassing or equally terrifying, and I don't want to suffocate others as much as I don't want others to bother me when they can't understand.

I am very intolerant of basic inconveniences. Each minor instance adds up to the classic *death by a thousand cuts*, and I can somehow deal better, emotionally and intellectually, with larger or more significant incidents than the more numerous smaller and irritating events that I have a passionate or rude reaction to. I never know how to react properly and can only be mature or wise in hindsight or retrospect. The moment something happens I am always more likely to be unreasonable and afraid. I cannot overcome this.

I have some idea of things I really want or need that would help me. Things that many take for granted or commonly speak of feel hard to admit because I am in a more desperate situation than others; they are harder to come by for me, and everything has a greater weight or immediacy. I can only ever have a partial truce with fear and the difficulty of life. I offer no true reconciliation to overcome the problems in life (again) either emotionally or intellectually. I think too many things are more difficult than we wish, or they are insurmountable, yet I don't accept liquidation or giving up either—which doesn't make me feel any better, clearly, and while less dishonest than false hope it offers only wallowing depression or aimless anger. Or other wearying emotions.

I vent my frustrations because I'm filled with hot air and I always overthink—I've never known not overthinking—and not venting will cause me more distress. Most talk on self-pity is cruel and disdainful, and I have always thought it mean in the majority of cases, especially mine, because I have always been self-pitying. The idea that I could not be (pitiable) and could instead embody some strength of spirit or resolve is puerile. People will say to others in similar situations as mine that they "don't know how you cope, I'd rather die than live like that."

This is not a compliment and it's also foolish. You don't get a choice. If you were born in the same situation you'd likely react in a similar way, as anyone else might; and I don't cope with my life as some noble and stoic effort. Yet one isn't allowed to be self-pitying in the common opinion. It's permissible, somehow, for others to despair at me or my situation, but I have to be strong and steadfast, despite how difficult that actually is—as if for their sake, because if I were not I might be annoying or frightening.

I wish to be strong in declaring what I need—though this can be uncomfortable for others. This is easy enough for me because I'm indulgent, so if I'm asked, I can say firmly what my needs are—impossible as they are or not. My pressing concern is being afraid most of the time, of my health and my fate, and just wanting emotional or loving support. I have good friends to talk to and confide in, family, but I will always experience an inescapable loneliness. Being vulnerable, disabled, ill, I'm in a unique situation even considering others who are ill—given the allowance that we are all special cases. The past couple years—due to Covid—have only made everything worse, with remoteness and health. It's too much to deal with. I just wish for people close to me who can stay with me, keep me safe, and secure me some happiness.

⁂ INTELLECTUAL INFLUENCE AND HISTORY

Alexis de Tocqueville and Montesquieu spoke the truth about many things.

I have a cautious and ambiguous attitude when it comes to what is *influential*. I can account it to a perceived linguistic confusion and my being autistically slippery with the definition.

People who praise these men overstate their authentic influence, or rather an influence perceived as and promulgated accurately. They may be well-known but it is a superficial while significant point that they aren't generally considered in a way that's accurate with respect to what they, individually, intended and wanted—as is the fate of many famous writers that I can't offer much of a solution to besides *read better*. The "liberalism" promoted by their disciples, is by accounts very illiberal—and Montesquieu, etc, might only be embarrassed by how dictatorial, unjust, and disappointing modern 'liberal democracies' are. The influence of individuals who wrote thick books with big ideas is often overstated; their influence is in most cases purported, attested to, but deviates significantly from anything they'd have wanted. Marx, Montesquieu, we must feel sorry for you—some stuff went down. Tolstoy's account of history, stating that *history's essential question still remains unanswered*, that it's hard to say how men and intellectual activity influence events, is probably true.

People who dislike Montesquieu or other historical figures who wrote and had fun ideas don't often know them very well, and commit the same folly as their supporters in grouping others together with various, apparently similar individuals whom they are not similar to at all upon close inspection—only sharing a few key influences. Few people, educated or not, dismiss or even praise an intellectual with actual knowledge; we catalogue them ineptly, either for convenience or from indolence.

More importantly, most people don't read at all. How can we say de Tocqueville was truly influential when most real (let's repeat the word again and see how annoying it gets) 'influence' is not the result of successful manifestos or individual power, but the mixed passions and emotions of people and institutions within 'the brutishness of events'?

It would be untrue and crude to say that de Tocqueville and Montesquieu were either greatly influential or didn't influence us at all—but the latter statement would be closer to the truth if we had to pick one. It would be better if they were *influential*, probably, maybe.

My tepid opinion is that de Tocqueville could simply say 'I told you so' considering the failures of our democracies, especially with respect to the USA, and Montesquieu would be completely horrified by but likely, somehow, unsurprised by most major historical despotic events post-1755, where people as diverse as Maximilian Robespierre, John Maynard Keynes, and President Mohammad Khatami speak of them.

> This civilisation is best described by the renowned French sociologist Alexis de Tocqueville, who spent some two years in the U.S. in the 19th century and wrote the valuable book entitled *Democracy in America*, which I am sure most Americans have read.
>
> Well, I don't think that's the case. I've taken this book around with me for the last few years and have asked many Americans . . . and have yet to meet one.
>
> [Khatami]

Will reading more solve our problems? Probably not. I doubt Boeing executives reading Spinoza will truly reform, but it's a comforting fantasy.

☻ Eternally Uniquely Silly

There's a nonsense modern trend where people feel the current age is uniquely censorious, regularly deeming people *persona non grata* for things previously viewed as harmless—a world past is seen as less puritanical or less likely to offend, ban things, or find one guilty for various sins. I refuse to use the currently popular modern euphemisms for this.

I don't think it surprising, as if anything really is, for people to view life so anachronistically. They act, somehow, as if they could say and do more in the 1980s or 1990s than they could today, and this is quantitatively false at least. The present day gives us the technological ability, not just the cultural permissibility, to *say more* than at any other time; one's opinions and inane talk are advertised to the world more greatly than in any other period of history. Much conspiratorial talk goes into who or what allows us a say, and large corporations are an obvious threat, but not for such rudimentary goals as promoting brief agendas—if they have any consistent ones able to be comprehended by most, who think only in tacky polemics. What I care more about is the sense of scale. As if one, as an average individual with internet access, not living in a regime that actively murders journalists, somehow has less of a say, or is somehow made a pariah, pilloried, or censured, more so than any time previously where you would be more likely to end up on trial, in prison, exiled or executed, for crimes now considered entirely noncriminal and acceptable discourse. I feel terrible about the hardships and poverty of the present day, but not in this way. Most opinions or behaviours that are actually risky and dangerous today are not—if I have to give an example: common right-wing opinions found online as abundantly as cats. One is especially and entirely not *silenced* for controversial opinions when these people appear headlined in syndicated newspapers, have multiple book deals, television specials, or popular podcasts able to broadcast their voices to thousands of adoring sycophants. A great majority of opinions perceived as controversial, that may be easy targets of attack and scorn, aren't ever, actually, removed. It's a wonderful grift for the well-off to feign impoverishment or conspiracies against them (while still speaking on this from an incredibly popular platform), to then bolster a career with the new identity of the edgy thinker saying the unsayable stuff said everywhere already. This especially becomes a clear joke once one sees who is actually at risk of real harm and death for an opinion, or for merely existing. A key definitional thing about people who are truly silenced or removed is that we don't fucking hear from them.

I don't want or be insulting. People are still killed for innocuous talk perceived as grievous sin, and I despair for the modern world with its litany of insoluble problems and dangers—including the conveyance and accruing of cogent information and knowledge, poverty; there's forever enough terror. I will not underestimate the trouble with modern technology and corporatism. With all this, it's more insulting when the insulated and easygoing pretend to real victimhood thinking they can't speak when they do so copiously, irresponsibly, all the damn time. Many would benefit from less expression—instead we have overwhelming pressures to *express ourselves*. Still, conflicting, in a world of many mansions and paradoxes, we can easily say this to the annoying or to terrorists: we get enough. Less so for those still assassinated for tame conversation, subject to real violence and not just mild criticism. Yet I'm still not sure how to get through to pretenders. I don't have much time for real argument or action, nor to distinguish between the false and the real victims; and executioners may be obvious if one thinks of the scale and quality of actual consequences. But reality won't conveniently alter popular comforts.

All this is a tired, similar reflection to older people bemoaning the young for indolence, or insolence, being workshy or undisciplined, which was a common opinion older generations had of their offspring in ancient times and has persisted for every generation since. Young folk in the 1790s were terribly rude and violent, and did not respect their elders. Young folk after WW1 did not respect the sacrifices made by . . .

It's a canard. And I'm certainly not novel or bright for pointing this out, given that it's laughably obvious and unoriginal. That still doesn't stop smarter individuals from believing intrinsic, essentially metaphysical and immutable characteristics exist depending on one's date of birth or nationality, where we still believe an ahistorical account of being uniquely, specially beleaguered victims today, with problems so novel and special. In part, modern problems are new and we can't seamlessly borrow pithy sayings from past figures, or even stronger investigations of social history, to explain and comprehend new set pieces. We can at least, or should at least, realise that people in the past thought and acted on similar prejudices. We might then only rearrange similar anxieties of a doomed and unstable world, similarly echoed rhetoric; and superstitions and stupidity certainly have not gone away. In regards to their quantity, given the number of the population and the quicker transference of false information, superstitions and lies—innocent, ridiculous, or terrifying—are more abundant than ever. In regard to their quality, lies remain about as untrue as ever. *The steady rate of filth.* We can rely on people from every corner and division, stripe and league, every denomination, of whatever taxonomy, to foster in their ranks consistent silliness, stupidity, or looming horror.

Unlike me, who is very smart and never so foolish.

☽ LIBERTY, APATHY, PITY

I was in hospital yet again. I'm not sure how beneficial it was, and my psychological health has suffered, due to world events but also my usual overthinking and my condition.

As a short reminder: any article, by anyone, educated or not, speaking of 'liberty' or 'freedom', pontificating on the successes and failures of scientific advice and policy, mildly conspiratorial about the loss of said liberties, but somehow completely silent on the matter of vulnerable and disabled people living through a pandemic ... is useless except as material to deride and to oppose. There's lots of articulate and inarticulate talk about policy being 'fundamentally inconsistent with liberty and individual dignity', where the *healthies* complain about disruption to their lives because of inept government policy regarding this pandemic, or talk from apparently 'progressive' voices who might sometimes be obtuse but are taken to be, somehow, a more pressing threat than the dominant conservatism or outright creeping fascism.

It comes at a cost when the speakers fail to note those who are genuinely most affected by a suppression of liberty or justice—who are not accounted for or even known. These are the voices of comfortable people tilting at windmills while others are left to starve and rot.

What is more fundamentally inconsistent with liberty? Not allowing anyone to behave recklessly in public, even if the rules are incompetently and strictly enforced, or allowing the apathetic and blithe public to run rampant and free to harm vulnerable people without much thought? Freedom from harm should be more important than the freedom to harm, surely? We can obviously object to despotism and overreach, yet recent policies to curtail this pandemic in Western countries, if described as despotism for those who've historically faced it, could be seen as laughably lenient and forgiving. You haven't faced any true regulation or restriction at all, and you certainly could not cope living the lives of people you revile or forget even exist.

This battle is lost. Apathy and the desire to avoid inconvenience matters more to the population than the life of a few disabled whiners. The atmosphere, the mood of the entire culture, is so thoroughly dominated by requirements set against making life less treacherous that there's little we can do to manage this planet for suitable habitation. I can only try to weather it. I'd rather not give up entirely, but the world will not get any better.

You can forgive my pessimism because I still enjoy what's good in life. What's good is far more precious, for it's outweighed so much by everything else.

There is not really such thing as a 'disability community'. There are smaller groups of supportive people and activists but any united idea of community is fanciful. Some may have some modicum of recognition and can support a cause or do some good work, but many more are entirely forgotten by everyone, left to fend for themselves and die genuinely alone.

I'm asked again by some how I cope with my condition. If I'm in a bad mood I might say that most couldn't, then. I barely do. Most who I know, compared to my own situation, live lives with a great abundance of opportunity and choice while I do not; I am essentially an invalid and will die without help, and I have to querulously accept a grim reality.

I can then be accused, I repeat, of indulgent self-pity; but by the admission of most I talk to, they *couldn't cope with it*. There are weaklings in good health. So am I allowed to be self-pitying if what I receive, when I bluntly describe myself, is sadness and distress? Maybe instead I can be arrogant and rude about their run of good luck, the tepidity of their hopeful, comforted lives, and the pettiness of their daily routines. I don't buy common alternatives regarding strength and fortitude: they apply better to prime specimens and liars.

I am concerned and pessimistic because (in a reference that will please friends), frankly, I *do* give a damn. My brand of pessimism comes from failed hope, I am morose or solemn and jaded because when examining my lot I am left feeling upset and enraged at an injustice, realising I can do little about it, but then unable to be accommodating and so regularly oscillating between cold acceptance and feverish terror. We do not cope with life. We are stuck within a favourite phrase of mine: *the perplexity of contending passions*.

I have good friends whom I can speak to and 'trauma dump' with paragraphs of heavy text, I can accept some grounded sensualism of friendship, but my mind is in a pit. Much of my upset comes from what is happening outside my control. I can't do as much because others are being callous, because life is inaccessible and inadequate, and what clear-sighted desires I do have are too difficult to fulfil if I am a solitary ill person dealing with significant events—where I can only wait for others to act and all I may do is beg.

Long notes or writing a book about myself and the phenomenology of chronic illness may do something to vent, but I think I can be forgiven how irritable and embittered I am.

I like to be childish and mischievous, but it's veneer—window dressing. I don't deal with life or my emotions very well most days, but being open about it is better than being opaque. Sometimes I remain closed, and I will choose to remain alone, and not reach out. I spend a lot of time being physically alone. But this is eventually corrosive, as much as it is good to escape crowds and noise. That might be a shallow reflection but it's no less poignant or true, and importantly I lack the infrastructure to better survive it.

If I talk about it, at least people can know that I'm not entirely lost at sea.

🥀 And Soon: Nothing More Terrible, Nothing More True

I'm apologetic to friends because in being honest about myself and my situation I dampen the mood. I speak with palliative care therapists about my prognosis and my emotional well-being, and I get a response that would entertain me if I weren't still overly-emotional: that I'm overqualified and over-read, so that I have a cogent grasp of how I am a very ill person not coping with life too well. Very nice.

I'm investing too much in an abstract idea of a relationship, because I somehow see this as what I want to better cope with things, and I think this is selfish, because I'm then roping someone into my own mess, but I'm unwilling to give up on the opportunity as failure means more to me. I'm acutely aware of young people lamenting their failures while they have whole decades worth of chances and time that I don't, so I envy them. It's then, still, more difficult when it takes more effort for me to get to know someone, be open about who I am and what's happening, and this will

SPECIOUS STUFF

turn most away; it's rare if they have some understanding of the reality and willingness to care.

They have this wealth of opportunity ahead of them, with the chance to live and work well and follow possibilities (if the economy doesn't tank any further or the world doesn't explode)—and the idea of asking someone to be open to something, some-thing more rather than nothing, just asking for a chance when others are so busy and have their own life . . . Is that rude? Or restrictive and unfair?

My health will only get worse and I'm already rather inactive, I don't have the ability to travel too far or live the lives of my peers—those whom I'm so jealous of when they go out in the world. How am I supposed to ask for something? Subtext says I do, here, anyway. The past years increasingly curtail what I can do, but I want to be brave. I hope I might find something.

September 2022

DISTRUST AND EXPERTISE

FIRST, I HAVE to give some credit to the philosopher Vlad Vexler, who I recommend as a sound analyst of political philosophy, as well as the late Bernard Williams—of whom Vexler is also an admirer. I can't claim to have much in the way of original thought and I repeat from memory some of what they might also say, or would hopefully agree with. So I give some due thanks to them.

In today's society people are pressured to 'generate knowledge', talking often, expressing themselves, self-styling, affirming: essentially advertising themselves and their identity long before the real accumulation of knowledge and reflection occur. At some level we can't begrudge this, and I'm really one to talk. Yet this is troubling considering people's moral motivations to commit violence. Most of us don't know precisely how to accumulate knowledge. People feel they must express themselves first, instead. This is, likely, worse than it used to be, due to technological, cultural, and social developments. It results in the proliferation of diffuse ideas and ideologies or a greater, dissociated scale of ideas and action that will be much more difficult to regulate or ever control using previous methods. The implications are anti-democratic—further democratic degradation, despotism, more conflict and violence.

Experts deal with this about as well as the public, which means not very well at all. They are pressured, consciously or implicitly, to speak grandly on things they know little or nothing about. Staying in one's lane becomes difficult, when it is sometimes advantageous to actually do that and not fear the limitations of one's knowledge or deferring to others. When experts, and not just the public, feel such a need—an almost righteous, narcissistic or otherwise arrogant compulsion—to comment about what they don't know (always a common phenomenon, though not so exaggerated in the past), this has wide implications—many of which are worrying or detrimental.

Speaking of expertise in general, academic expertise, people with some real brilliance or quality, or at least a perceived intellectual weight—such experts are commonly invited to speak about anything on the basis that they are knowledgeable people. But their knowledge is limited to a specific area; they are not omniscient. And many speak embarrassingly about what they know less about. When invited to express an opinion, experts are valuable. Especially valuable when they really are intelligible and cogent on a particular subject—and speak with confidence. When asked a question one doesn't have a good answer to, or which one has no answer to, it is more important than many think to say one does not know something, and to defer one's expertise. When experts talk outside their realm of competence, and do so poorly, they obscure what they are genuinely knowledgeable about. It is much more difficult for others to recognise real expertise when an expert expresses obtuse opinions that have a diffusing and dissociating effect. This is more important than many think.

Expertise matters. Without it we have a crisis of trust and a real threat to democracy. Speaking with Bernard Williams, we might say that democracy is bound to the practical virtue of truthfulness. And associated with trustworthy institutions. There exists a great crisis of trust in institutions today, as the world grows and things move very quickly, resulting in the proliferation of conspiracy theories and, further, greater conflict and possible violence. This is, in part, a self-inflicted wound as institutions struggle with how to conceive of themselves in contemporary society, with the greatly increasing demands and contradictions of a developing modern society, and this struggle contributes to distrust, made worse by the social climate and other nefarious interventions.

Experts talking about anything they like within this climate are more dangerous than they may consciously imagine. We can, or should, have a wide tolerance for speech (even destructive speech), but the contention here is the responsibility of the expert we fail to consider, or for that matter its wider implications. Experts talking about anything and everything, when their realm of expertise is deep but narrow, renders their virtues less clear and makes them appear less trustworthy. With the result that experts generally are then perceived as less trustworthy. Our struggle to make sense of things is compounded not just by the irresponsible talk of experts idly pontificating outside their domains, but by societal and technological demands.

Wide talk is sometimes useful, but there is, in part, less real dialogue and collaboration when we are subjected to a narcissistic broad expertise. People struggle to understand when an expert is truly knowledgeable and how, or when, to defer to whom. Greater societal distrust is a crisis for democracy—a lack of intellectual humility has troubling implications.

These thoughts are partly abstract, but they indicate that we are dealing with a moral climate influenced by the practical, industrial, technological demands of society.

Which means, moreover, that solutions to some of our worst problems are not easy, though perhaps they would have been easier to rectify or mitigate in the past—in, again, a different social, technological, and cultural climate.

Many of us, whether or not experts in some field, wish to apply generalised or abstract rules to the world, predicated on how we think actors and powers should behave rationally, or based on pre-conceived notions, with very broad demographic and logistical considerations—rather than considering very particular and individual ways that nations, societies, or leaders, behave depending on their local and regional history, or their acute idiosyncrasies. This is closer to a game with set rules, or a formula, a scheme, a plan, than it is to reality. One cannot routinely apply a general rule of politics that would function in one place—say, the USA, or Russia, viewing the nations at a low resolution from far above—rather than more intimately investigating local developments and history. This is a type of cultural narcissism, manifest in American foreign affairs (consider American leftists thinking nations are only reactive to American activity, and without their own domestic considerations and history) or typical of Europeans when viewing America (snobbery), a projection of their own values and ideas, deemed obvious and evident, that makes Europeans think things should work according to their own criteria and worldview, without a more intimate reflection.

Responsible experts in specific fields exist. And we do better if we act with a greater intellectual responsibility to know this. The world is uncertain and trust has become rarer and rarer. It should still exist, and untactful relativism is an easy tool in the arsenal of autocrats and dictators—just as strident propaganda is. But truth, as Democritus once said, is in the depths. It isn't easy and requires prudence and responsibility—both resources in short supply across the world. We fail if we don't consider how to navigate this world, and mitigate its dangers.

May 2023

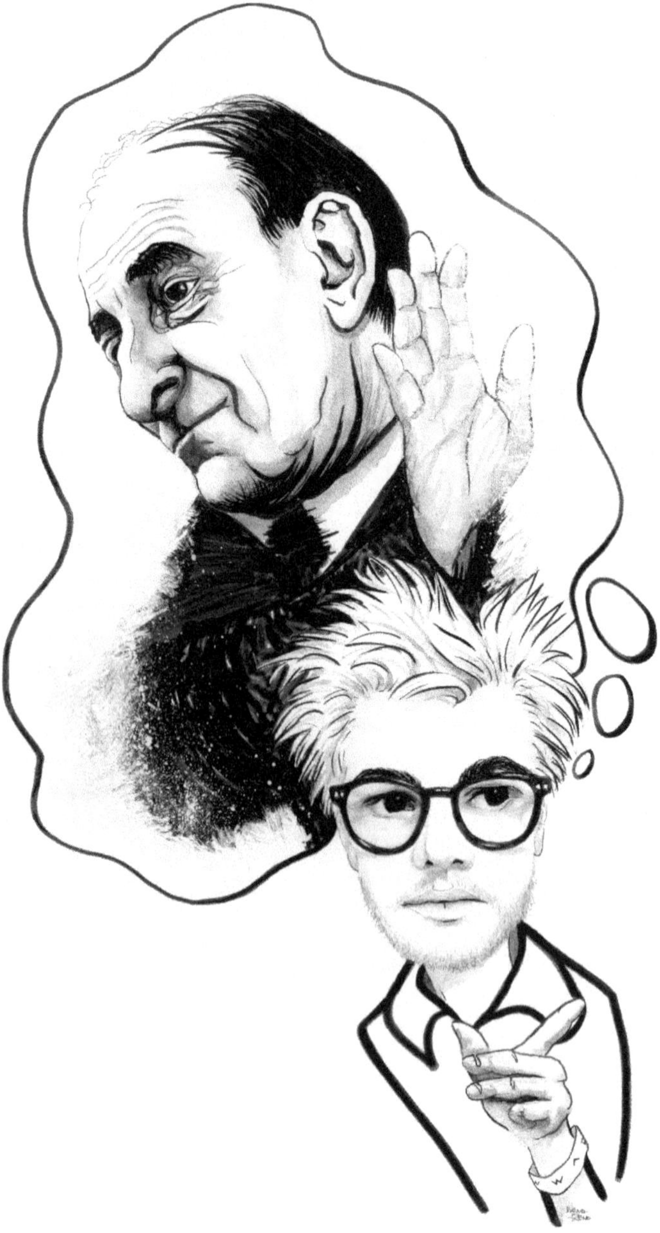

A Brief Note About Aronian
Liberalism

RAYMOND ARON (1905–1983) was a complex man. French sociologist, philosopher, professor, journalist, Jew. He is someone I have read widely, a hefty hardcover of his *Memoirs* is among my favourite books. The primary complication with Aron is the difficulty in ascribing an easy political identity to him—as is so desired by many. Where one places him politically says more about one's own position. He had a broad influence and was a man who, during his life, held many friendships, acquaintances, and antagonisms across the board.

Disregarding bad readings of him, hasty declarations on his allegiances, aspersions with respect to his character or personality, I want to note what Aron, as a cautious, discerning, humanistic voice can offer. I don't necessarily care to write a biography about him—that's already been done. I could rightly be accused of laziness for not digging deeper into his life and work, especially as I take issue with a generalised understanding of Aron and his history. I instead want to suggest, mildly, briefly, without some heavy analysis in an extended volume, an attention to his possible meaning or legacy.

My crude coping mechanism whenever someone is mean and troubling politically is to think: 'What Would

Aron Do?' And I know Aron is smarter, more astute, more sensible and level-headed than most commentators on the internet, so I feel immensely superior, incredibly *built different*, as I and my fellow kids say.

I don't want to appear glib . . . because this is a man who died in 1983 and having some emotional attachment to a dead intellectual to make up for my own failings could prove troubling if I were not careful or critical, but Aron was, by much academic and anecdotal judgement, both more sensible and sane than his contemporaries, and I feel an almost justified nostalgia for a type of person with both a level of fame and scholarly expertise that is much rarer to find in a unified combination today.

I like to say my attraction is detached from cults of personality revolving around figures with easily advertised, proselytised ideas because, one would hope, knowing Aron's ideas and personality means having a critical, doubtful, cautious and discerning perspective—not an unreasoning reverence.

But here also is my own insecurity. I am thoroughly opposed to forms of hero worship and messianism, yet this means I am too critical of myself in my ability to just like and enjoy something. I'm always doubting my own raw enjoyment of even trivial things, lest I somehow become a nasty cultist or too intellectually complacent. And I should afford myself some levity instead. I want to present a vague idea and hope it finds some purchase.

A BRIEF NOTE ABOUT ARONIAN LIBERALISM

Here is a brief outline of some social, cultural, and political issues we currently face: if one is complacent and can't conceive of how 'reactionary elements' will . . . react, if there isn't the creation of better material conditions to mitigate problems, or a legal system is easy to exploit, it's little surprise when democracy becomes weak and authoritarian elements flourish.

Convincing people, via argument, to become morally improved is far less effective than incentivising better behaviour by creating more prosperous or tenable conditions. If where one lives is poor and shit, some people will react poorly—either in their intellectual conceptions or their actionable, practical methods.

This doesn't remove all agency from fascists and bad actors, as if harmful people are produced solely by a bad environment, yet even conceding these people are horrible, and *reactionary*, how do we think they will react to bad conditions and a perceived lack of responsibility for the world as it is from the vantage of those in positions of power—or how do people otherwise react to arrogance? How does anyone effectively respond to people with a list of many grievances, authentic or not, in a way that isn't merely accusatory, and practically inadequate? One should know how poorly they themselves respond to hostile shaming and accusations, justified or not. If our goal is behaviour change, what is the most tactful way to achieve this? Emphasising the great divisions of society and identity is perhaps not the best way to get someone, if they can at least be saved from monstrous ideas, to empathise with others they otherwise cannot understand or share exact experiences with. We can forget the most violent demands, one can't murder half a population for their voting habits and miraculously solve injustice. We don't create sustainable change by abrogating responsibility (especially if one is in power). Political opponents don't exist exclusively outside of us as aliens. They are a problem we have to face and not simply disparage and scorn. Whether that is through overt violence and security, or a better legal system, or the hopeful demand to foster conditions that would stop people from becoming fascists and despots in the first place. I present this line of questioning to account, I'd hope, for a better strategy and personal reflection.

Aron can't necessarily speak for us in 2023, nor could he have foreseen the exact path of societal development, but he can maybe speak to us generally about what our aims should be, our attitudes, or how we may compose ourselves politically.

Many in politics, across the whole spectrum as it is commonly perceived, have a sort of *Fukuyama-esque* arrogance where they think their position is entirely obvious and doesn't need unsentimental, proper defending; or, rather, is somehow historically inevitable. Some may want to think they're past *end of history* thinking, but their dispositions and attitudes don't portray this.

Once one believes this, they're not just intellectually or teleologically weak, but an arrogance in their own position means they don't comprehend how to properly, strategically, face an opposition, know what an enemy is, or properly defend their own intellectual infrastructure.

An arrogance in her own position meant Hilary Clinton's infamous 'deplorables' comment backfired. The people she spoke of may well, technically, in some admission, say deplorable things or believe in some horrible ideas. But by most observations it still backfired. No matter how truthful one may think the language was, it was tactically ineffective. The admonishment was worn as a badge of honour; Clinton has little idea why fascists exist or at least how to react to them; or prevent their multiplication. Equally, leftists, anti-authoritarian or authoritarian, are just as useless and dithering in their practical organisation or intellectual consistency. Their language amounts to the same proportion of blame, and a resentful reaction is unsurprising. It's not so much about being correct, I could reasonably say that my political opponents are terrible people or at least have terrible ideas, but this is complaining—not effective change. We can forgive ourselves for outbursts against the most horrible of people, especially when they have harmed us, or traumatised us, and we're not expecting people to speak and act politely. If impropriety works on occasion, it's welcomed. The real contention, here, is efficacy.

It's tragic, and terrible, when reactionary, discriminatory, anti-democratic and fascistic tendencies proliferate— as they are festering and have been for a while across the world. It's alarming, but not surprising. Something like Brexit, resentment-driven, often simplistically yearning, often plainly xenophobic, shouldn't have surprised people. The rise of Viktor Orbán, and other similar personalities, is also equally terrible, but not surprising. Not many are facing these issues in, again, an effective or efficient way. Bad political results still surprise people. Why? A small proportion of this surprise is our own complacency. Few ask *why exactly is this person horrible*? They just know they are. Or they rationalise reasons, accept convenient messaging, without a more uncomfortable investigation. Worse, they suppose, again, that their position and the position of a rival is obvious, now believing their strategy is fine. Without getting to the root or exploring the difficult dimension of stepping into an opponent's shoes, it's unlikely we can truly combat things. Being righteously correct, in a moral dimension, only goes so far. It doesn't suppose great tactical knowledge, like a military commander knowing the correct steps to reach a goal. I contend that good strategy and tactics are vanishingly rare, while feeling correct doesn't require the same effort. I don't suppose, either, as if it needed to be said, that I can be a commander or point them out, but I at least have the confidence to say things aren't going very well.

A continent like Europe has always had to deal with nationalistic tendencies, and a push towards a perceived variety of federalism or pluralism would eventually receive some reply, even if that reply is unwelcome, uninformed, or mean-spirited. The EU is far from perfect; it benefits some more than others, and when conditions are poorer in many places, it's easier to blame particular easy targets rather than fix on any real issues, which will be equivocated, and especially so by non-benevolent media and politicians.

Aron, who was always of a cosmopolitan spirit, while still an advocate for France, wished for a greater, friendly co-operation between European powers. With this, he was aware of nationalistic tendencies and the difficulty of ever overcoming them. He hardly couldn't be. He was a Jew in Europe, witnessing the rise of fascism, and someone who sounded the alarm early, too. The situation since is not the same, yet we can still notice centuries-old antagonisms and preoccupations. A European project needs to be better orchestrated if we want to have a closer, yet fairer relationship, politically and economically, while recognising a homogenisation will cause some backlash and resentment. It's a balancing act, and nuance dies in politics.

A BRIEF NOTE ABOUT ARONIAN LIBERALISM

A weakness of Aron, almost, is how he'd be so meticulous and see issues from so many different angles, an "impressionist's approach", with so many things happening at once (while still maintaining his own stance), yet his recognition of this complexity is beyond many who don't necessarily have the time to sit and reflect, and it is then difficult to translate someone who is complex, muted, and considerate, into easy language and comforting slogans. Bad ideas are easier to translate into clichés and appealing propaganda. We aren't as good at translating discerning ideas into digestible euphemisms, which is partly why better political philosophers don't have good solutions: they just can't be implemented very easily. And successful politicians can be, we say arrogantly, stupid people appealing to stupid people.

A European project failing to recognise these issues is unsurprising, and our worst tendencies are always unsurprising. If we are wanting to be more complex, one still has to deal with uncomplicated people who are immediately hostile or unappreciative, and we rarely have much idea of how to most optimally deal with them.

The distancing and, in popular vocabulary, *othering* of political opponents as ontologically evil, entirely aberrant, where one abrogates any responsibility for their opponents' existence or grievances, and dehumanises evil, is apparent with overzealous people on the left, and very obviously on the right, and sometimes less so among 'liberals', or at least liberals who don't fall for a Fukuyama-style, or, inversely, an occasionally Marxist conceit of thinking their version of politics and history is inevitable. Leftists have commonly believed their ideas are obviously, axiomatically true, and even, again, historically inevitable, rather than true but with robust defences—which means it is easier to *other* and distance your opponents, create a sense of righteous superiority, to become practically and logistically ineffective, and one rationalises any falsehoods or lack of coherence. If anything, among more consistent 'liberals', these tendencies, or attitudes, are less common.

It's a common conceit on the left to believe "liberalism" is closer to fascism (and thus evil) thanks to a flimsy conceptualisation of the political spectrum, and always closer to that bane than their own ideas, which are somehow obviously not bad and won't be exploited . . . Aron observed, in the helpful words of Clive James, that "during the Weimar Republic the left intelligentsia hated capitalism, and hence social democracy as well, far too much to think that Nazism could be worse."

The hostile pre-occupation with capitalism as an economic motor, for all of capitalism's flaws and injustices, meant a lack of imagination. Things could get much worse. Aron's defence of liberal democracy is always critical. It always had to be criticised in detail, but the complete abandonment of it was a less preferable choice open to further exploitation, and, for him, not the best way towards social justice. This is aesthetically unpopular, seemingly a resignation to a least bad option instead of an aspiration for an idyllic best. A warning against dreams becoming nightmares, anti-Icarus. One could regard it as pessimistic, yet political movements have always had confused relationships with a pessimistic assessment of the world as it is, yet a sometimes magically optimistic idea of their own ambitions and ability. If we are more humble, we can maybe recognise how to practically oppose the worst of human tendencies. Aron adopted a less-popular role. He said himself, "I am sure this makes me a reasonable man—and yet know that it is often the dreamers, not the reasonable men, who change society. There is a danger in being reasonable, in being excessively lucid. There is an important place in the social order for impatient people, and I have at times been impatient myself. But France, and the world, have no lack of dreamers. My function, the function of the reasonable man, has fewer practitioners—and it is important, too."

Instead of holding consistent aspirations, regimes as well as personal ideas need to be understood as inconsistent and hypocritical. People have always created history in the name of ideas, but the history they have created has never faithfully reflected their ideas. And some ideas can easily lend themselves to bad interpretations. Sometimes a democratically centrist, capitalist, liberal regime will be the present administrators most greatly opposed to fascism in a particular time and place, better equipped than leftists, and sometimes the opposite is true — variably, any of these political categories can fail to combat fascism and be ineffective, or counterproductive.

Part of this problem, our efficacy in resisting harmful ideas, is how people view the nature of their opponent. They can be correct on the very basic truth that something or someone is bad, but if this idea is very rudimentary (i.e you don't know your enemy), we find the problem of *othering* evil instead of recognising it more clearly and in its full human breadth and depth.

Leftists, commonly, don't understand liberalism—it's a buzzword insert for apparent misfortunes, sometimes a true indictment of diffuse liberal weaknesses, but hardly so categorically. So-called liberals and neoliberals, especially of an American persuasion, with definitions at cross-purposes with historical readings, also don't understand liberalism, or pluralism, or equality under the law—so much so that what they often espouse is illiberal, anti-democratic, or an institutional failure to uphold basic tenets of equality, liberty, and justice. Worse, the language of freedom is readily exploited by ultra- conservatives, and fascists, with policy directly opposed to equitable principles: banning books, exploiting and neglecting vulnerable people, voter suppression, significant financial and social inequity, etc. Everyone is inadequate both in practical scenarios as well as intellectually in their real knowledge of nebulous concepts, with too many personalised and caricaturised understandings. This doesn't mean I pin my allegiance solidly to the banner to say "I'm a liberal". I'm more concerned with the general as well as the acute misunderstanding of the political vocabulary, and the practical effectiveness in combating anti-democratic, despotic, and fascistic ideas. What I'd advise is the forgotten prudence and sceptical humility of Cold War liberals like Aron or Isaiah Berlin against the teleological arrogance and misguided optimism of post-Soviet neoliberalism and neoconservatism.

> The man who no longer expects miraculous changes either from a revolution or from an economic plan is not obliged to resign himself to the unjustifiable. It is because he likes individual human beings, participates in communities, and respects the truth, that he refuses to surrender his soul to an abstract ideal of humanity, a tyrannical party, and an absurd scholasticism ... If tolerance is born of doubt, let us teach everyone to doubt all the models and utopias, to challenge all the prophets of redemption and the heralds of catastrophe.
>
> [Raymond Aron, *The Opium of The Intellectuals*]

A BRIEF NOTE ABOUT ARONIAN LIBERALISM

Reading Aron's 1968 essay *Progress and Disillusion: The Dialectics of Modern Society*, in 2023, with the economic and social developments that have occurred since, a lazy reader could almost cherrypick quotations and passages to justify a stereotypical, caricaturist socialism. Aron suggests, entirely reasonably one might say, that the economic question *par excellence* is the organisation of wealth in society. Or, how to best use the limited resources available to us. And how most should concede that even if technology and industry necessitate a hierarchy, and act at odds with egalitarian principle, and very rich individuals may exist, if extant wealth is technically able and abundant enough to cover the relative needs of everyone to lead a comfortable living, with their relative needs fulfilled according to contemporary standards and costs—in other words, affording a living wage—this should be aspired to and negotiated, as well as other seemingly insoluble inequalities mitigated, with the hope that future social and technological orders we cannot predict will more successfully accept egalitarian principle. Unrest and violence are predictable if a regime can't realise economic and social needs, while a coherent or cogent revolutionary response is not so predictable. Order is provisional, and institutions are more fragile than we think. Industrial, technological societies, with the imperative of production, can never absolutely overcome the dissatisfactions they produce no matter how they are organised: whether according, superficially, to capitalist or communist rules.

Aron goes into greater detail on various social stratifications and the contradictions of modern society, but we can reasonably concede an easier narrative here.

Rather than respecting these cautions, modern deregulatory economics, austerity policies, and an inverted obsession with private property and privatisation have all proliferated instead of the acceptance of decent, indeed centuries-old egalitarian principles. Enough social movements and identities decry an industrial order and policy that may pay meagre lip-service to equality yet does not organise or distribute wealth in a fairer sense that is, perceptibly, logistically possible: technological and industrial progress is not compromising fairly enough with social and cultural demands. This isn't a communistic aim, these were the principles of a man accused of being a right winger. Not accepting Marxist *inevitabilities*, or noting that Marxist historicism and predictions of class struggle contain inaccuracies, is enough for some to be accused of anything. We can note that Aron respected Marx enough, knew the richness of his theory, and certainly read and investigated him more thoroughly than most self-described believers.

Aron disdained injustice and inequality, the overly-conservative nature of his country, and hoped that seemingly inscrutable racial, national, and historical antagonisms could somehow be treated and eventually overcome—even if he thought many proposed solutions were unlikely or unavailable, or they needed a longer convalescence. Accusations were levelled at him more for his emotional disposition—as an observer, not an outspoken activist, seemingly too cold and aloof. Aron's uncommon emotional outbursts were stronger for their rarity and their intimacy.

A cautious prediction today would see Aron noticing not just the inefficacies of progressive voices, but the contemptible failure of the proprietors of wealth to ensure a fairer society; entrenching divisions and rejecting inclusivity. The moderate right is hollow; the far-right promotes itself further; financial elites enrich themselves while the rest get by on less and less. Liberal dispositions appear weak and mediocre; leftist proponents dither and fail, and most are understandably distracted by social media and the overabundance of trivia. Popular voices, dreamers, speak of breaking free of this trap of *realism*, this seemingly incontestable situation where so many are powerless. I don't believe many of them, who by my reckoning appear seduced by easy temptations and phrases. Some of their visions, when not suffering from hankerings to Leninism or other passé, zombie ideologies, are noble and just—with an acute awareness of misfortune and a wish to alleviate it. As dreamers, I hope they can offer a better world, but at least heed warnings and know their true ability. They won't get so far if, like the archetypical philosopher, now the archetypical activist, they fall down the well with their head in the clouds.

For Aron, political choices weren't about what was best but about choosing what was preferable over what was detestable. Aron didn't aspire to pessimism, but contending with the disillusions and dissatisfactions of people faced with new events and the complications of history never has an easy or straight solution.

> ... the liberal believes in the permanence of humanity's imperfection, he resigns himself to a regime in which the good will be the result of numberless actions, and never the object of a conscious choice. Finally, he subscribes to the pessimism that sees, in politics, the art of creating the conditions in which the vices of men will contribute to the good of the state.
>
> [Raymond Aron, *The Opium of The Intellectuals*]

I don't expect a consistent, unified, and actionable political project to ever exist based on Aron's particular attitudes and ideas. I think other ideas are more tantalising and attractive, or sensible warnings won't likely be heeded. But we should say that I am more pessimistic than Aron himself. Aron saw societies in turmoil, the incompleteness of promised success, with less defensible injustices each day. With every advance, moral discrimination is more obvious and the pressure to move faster grows. Yet he did not despair for our future. It is harder today, especially for younger generations, to not despair at our surroundings and our future. What we might hope for, in my desperate attempt, is an understanding of Aron and his ideas as a wiser, almost paternal guide who explains how to, maybe, discerningly, yet dutifully contend with political misfortune and navigate our oppositions.

Aron is best as a critic and as someone offering a warning, so it might be in our interest to listen—and hopefully prevent future mistakes.

April 2023

WORSE THAN A CRIME

Author's Note: this essay started as an attempt to articulate, more for myself, my feelings on the attacks perpetrated by Hamas against Israeli civilians in October 2023, the Israeli response, and ethical/unethical responses common on social media. I am coy in commenting on events in the news as they happen, in writing, and my political thoughts are normally focused on past intellectuals and abstracting their ideas; possibly out of a sense of cowardice and the sense that too many people already speak on this issue. This particular conflict, with its history and the convolutions of identity involved, make most discourse more perilous. So I take care to repeat myself continually, out of a fear that anything I say will be understood poorly, by partisans of every variety involved. Part of this is selfish, and I could more easily point a reader in the direction of various political scholars or correspondents who would make the same points I do here, and with greater success. Many feel a need to speak on events, even if it's loud and overwhelming, but we can't begrudge them or stop them. Nor should we, really.

"It is worse than a crime, it is a mistake."—Charles Maurice de Talleyrand-Périgord.

WHEN A TRAGIC event occurs, in distant politics or in one's personal life, we should have an understanding of time being needed to properly express oneself, and the danger of trying to say too much too quickly; because explanations can feel like excuses when they are voiced too quickly, without reflection or a moment to breathe. Social

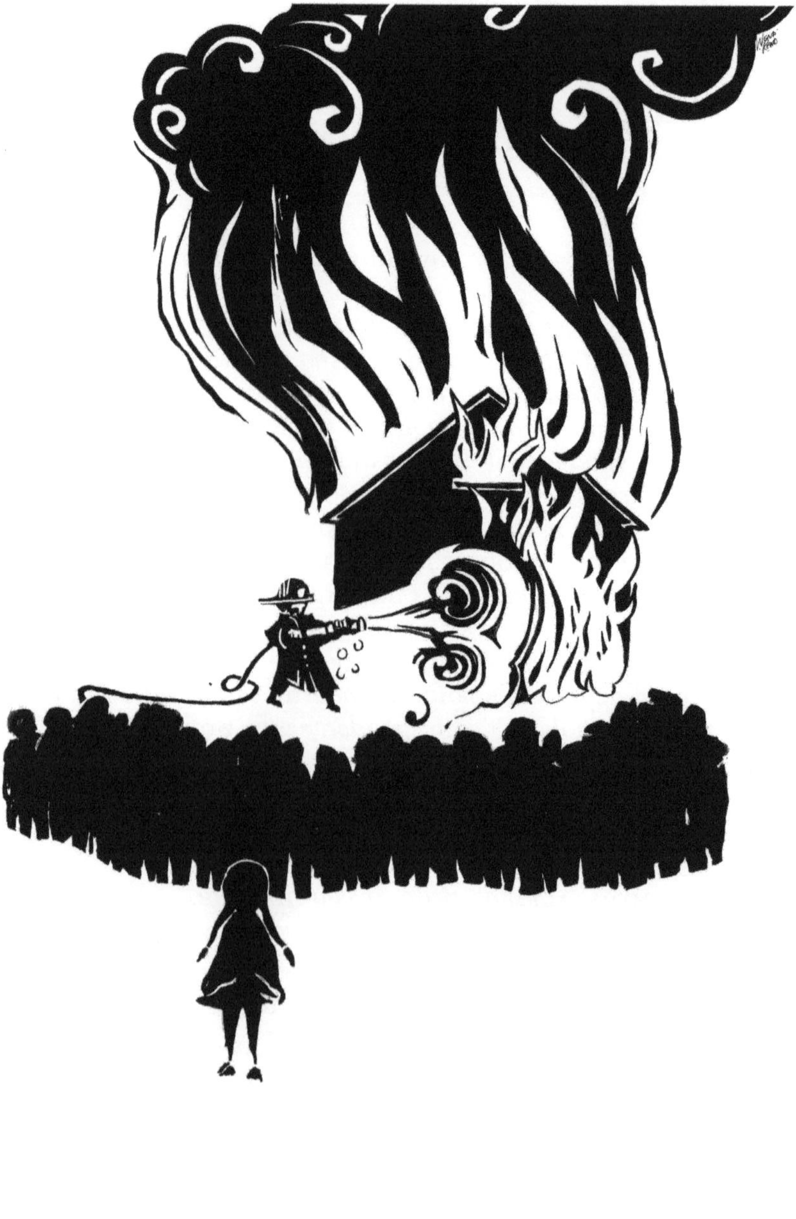

media worsens this situation, where the time we should afford during personal tragedy, from lamenting a loss, to then trying to explain why something has happened, is not allowed. In the fast-paced environment of social media we don't so easily afford this, we speak too quickly, and we don't reflect. This means we also behave immaturely, indulging in vices and prejudices, where the treatment of a serious conflict is turned into flag-waving and sectarian cant. This applies no matter where one's sympathies lie, with no matter what one eventually wants to happen, and no matter how one proportions responsibility or blame. As a tactical move it is not efficient or prudent to engage with serious politics in this way, nor is it a good ethical recommendation, and any lack of success will be unsurprising. Recognising how and when to say things, no matter what they are, is important. And just because one feels they are very correct, this does not stop them from imprudent speech, or imprudent actions, that may hinder their cause.

There is an attitude some have, when witnessing terrorism, even if one is judging a cause to be just, to express apologia and explanation before expressing sadness or grief, not affording themselves an interval and, more so in the environment of social media—where an obligation is felt to make declarations on anything instead of being quiet—there is little space for *moral time*: meaning, events require a temporal levity, you can't say everything at once. If the only liberating, emancipatory activity one thinks an oppressed group is capable of is indiscriminate violence against non-combatants (which is not only immoral, but strategically stupid), this is a belittling insult against said oppressed group, as if they are only capable of being brutish animals when faced with oppression, with no faculty or agency for coherent military or political operations. It's also a depoliticised position; it's not a political plan, or a strategy to produce a working governance or have any real policy at all. Violence, when required, as it is required by all states and political entities in some degree, needs a policy behind it, and preferably a longer-term thinking about how, after war and violence, one will be able to exist, and manage, politically—and not be vanquished by one's enemies or from within.

Anybody intentionally killing non-combatants is bad enough, not just as an immoral action but as a strategic blunder. Defending such violence becomes ridiculous as well as debased. Lazy critics of the position I've expressed may deem it naïve, as if I'm expressing some tepid liberal pacifism—which is wrong, and not what I'm doing. Both liberal democracies and revolutionary movements, or any political entity with state-like ambitions, often have to engage in violence—for their own defence, security, or liberation. The question is how. More pertinently, the question is how to prevent unintended consequences that may come from violence, which superpowers as well as revolutionary or counter-revolutionary groups often fail to do.

Some of the worst opinions on social media, after the start of the 2023 Israel-Hamas war, were hyper-identity focused, often Anglophone 'decolonial' views, that believe decolonial activity should naturally, as part of its revolutionary policy, express this sort of depoliticised violence against non-combatants, and that a just cause will validate such actions. As if revolt should necessarily engage in not just delimited, but unlimited violence. To briefly assess some of these arguments I will make use of common vocabulary.

Decolonisation, if it's a coherent theory and practice, needs to be constructive. If one is lazily studying Fanon (someone I have at least some admiration for), or some other popular theorist, or trying to produce a greater state of equity, are rape and murder viable methods to achieve decolonial aims, and will they produce a sustainable, eventually peaceful, prosperous way of living that is politically feasible? Can a group like Hamas somehow be a legitimate expression of conducive revolutionary practice? It would be *reactionary*, I think, to say so. Is not only apologising for murder, and eliminating distinctions between combatants and non-combatants, but glorifying murder, going to produce a sustainable political future? Religious fundamentalism would also preclude any group from being truly emancipatory; and is ruinous. Nor is fundamentalism only a reactive position, it is also an active position with distinct agency. Everyone bares some responsibility for their ideas and their actions, and how they conceive of others, even if we entertain that a group has comprehensible grievances. How any fashionable decolonial discourse may apply to Hamas is a different question to how it may apply, more legitimately, to other groups who don't hold not only reactive, but actively harmful racist positions. It should not take this much dialogue to say that Hamas are brutal and dangerous, and won't ever produce what Palestinians deserve. The positions of the coloniser and the colonised, the oppressor and the oppressed, are never permanent. History has enough potential for anyone to engage in terror; which cannot be justified by past events.

The use of force is an accepted reality for most serious political entities, but fundamentalist violence and atrocities are not congruent with turning a new leaf afterwards, somehow acting as an effective forward step towards a stable future or liberated prosperity. Atrocities are not pragmatic, at least in the long term, even if one cares nothing for altruism. This question applies to empires and to *oppressive* powers, to Israel, to Russia (whose only offering is violence), to the United States, or to any colonial administration, as much as it may to various oppressed groups, however they're organised or not, seeking whatever version of justice or emancipation (indeed, the question is arguably more significant for purported imperial powers. The current condition of Gaza is a classic example of a policy that is immoral and politically disastrous, by its primary authors—Israel). Violence may be necessary for any state, yet there are strong moral and tactical distinctions in how states, or any military force, should carry out violence, and those distinctions should not be cheapened.

Some, of many persuasions, might say it is politically viable and morally justified to intentionally kill non-combatants, which has been a technique employed for centuries. This doesn't recognise perverse incentives and one's own failings. It's a hubristic position and is bad in itself. The position superficially appears to be highly politically charged, but the encouraged violence isn't coherently politically focused and, I'd argue, is less politically viable regardless of morality. It might seem bold to claim, looking over history, that violence doesn't work. Violence is always a reality, and is often necessary. What can we say of the longevity of regimes engaged in unlimited violence? Unnecessary violence becomes impractical, rather than cynically profitable. Many regimes have fallen not only due to loss in a necessary conflict, but due to violence made in ignorance. When an enemy responds with overwhelming force, and commits its own vicious crimes and mistakes, this is unsurprising. If the aim, somehow, is to trigger an enemy to engage in overwhelming violence, that is a spiritually and intellectually impoverished position, and not a situation where anyone wins.

A few resort to conspiratorial views when a group that they support, or a relation to a group, commits atrocities, thinking as if all the rape and murder is a false-flag operation created as a pretence for agitation or war, rather than examining the failings of those they think are fighting for a just cause. No amount of just correctness and righteousness, if that can be conceded in some circumstance or another, prevents one from making a serious error, which is a tame way of describing the murder of civilians.

> Quite a few pro-Palestinian voices in the West are not condemning Hamas. Putting ethics side, this is a political mistake. It alienates a natural ally: pro-Palestinian Jewish Israelis, leaving them feeling pretty alone, as if not just their government but the world is against them.
> [Vlad Vexler]

A few vocal Anglophone leftists then 'outsource' this expression of violence, wishing that similar violence could occur in the US, against colonisers and oppressors—even indiscriminately against random targets. This process optimistically overestimates their own ability to produce organised violence and sustainable change, in a process of exaggerated abstract and magical thinking, and underestimates the obvious overwhelming response that would destroy them. Even if we entertain that a cause is a just and correct one, such abandonment of basic military practicality, just dreaming of violence for fun and catharsis, is a mistake and a trap. That's being as charitable as I can be, suggesting a just cause might, maybe, merit wanton violence, or that such an outburst of violence could be understood after long mistreatment. I'll be accused of being a pessimistic, hypocritical liberal for saying that indiscriminate violence is immoral, and not just bad planning. I may then be further accused, without much discretion, of siding with oppressive violence; as if I don't equally, if not more impatiently, condemn that as well for immorality, barbarism, and ignorance.

If an oppressive regime conducts itself in a way that provokes a terroristic response, and their own actions have involved significant destruction and death, this is also, in some regard, an unsound policy. It shows a lack of anticipation for how anyone may react to one's own actions or positions, and a lack of coherent preparation. It is a security mistake if one's exercise of power has disenfranchised civilians, killed civilians, and provoked a further growth in intolerant fundamentalism, just as much as it is immoral to have besieged and ruined lives.

Recently has been the worst informational environment on social media, for a number of reasons, including the mismanagement of popular social networks. I will labour the point: Hamas murdering non-combatants isn't just unethical, it's a political miscalculation and even, one could argue, and as I will repeat, depoliticised. If one thinks a free Palestine is a just cause (which I'd say it is), this doesn't justify intentionally murdering non-combatants, removing the distinction between combatants and non-combatants; which, to stress again, is not just a moral argument but a logistical and political one. If one's goal is a free Palestine, this is one of the worst ways to achieve it. And making excuses for it does not further the cause of Palestinian freedom.

If one's goal is the security and integrity of Israel, currently going through a democratic crisis and ceding to authoritarianism, the mistreatment of Palestinians is not just immoral on its own, but also a tactical ineptitude, a mistake, which costs the security of Israel and its citizens, and Jews worldwide who are spuriously blamed for the actions of the Israeli state. Indiscriminately bombing Palestinians is not just bad, it's foolish.

I'm not sure if anyone can express a truly serious, succinct opinion on the history, present, and possible future of Israel/Palestine in under 2 minutes. Alistair MacIntyre said that if one is ever talking about Israel/Palestine, then that is the only thing they should speak about in that conversation, and it's not a subject where wild tangents are useful or one can speak casually. All global conflicts produce various misunderstandings and bad interpretations. Israel/Palestine has the unfortunate tendency to produce even greater misunderstandings, and those responding to it will be even more specially dense. As a modern conflict it is more specially insoluble, and there is an incredibly small chance that peace could finally be attained, besides in the very long-term, unless some solution comes out of left-field which nobody has yet foreseen.

Ukraine/Russia is a conflict I actually could try to explain in under 2 minutes, and I will share philosopher Vlad Vexler's summation: An imperial project which has nothing to offer (except violence) invading a country which wants to be free (from said violence), motivated by regime security and a quasi-mystical desire to overturn global arrangements.

I couldn't express an opinion on Israel/Palestine so succinctly and quickly, if I want to be serious about it, no matter where I land.

Does Israel deserve to exist as a state? I give no special credit for any state to exist, meaning Israel has as much of a right to exist as Britain, France, India, Nigeria, North Korea, or any other country. When any of these states do something I disapprove of, I don't believe they should, impractically, cease to exist; I wish they'd simply not be so bad.

Does Israel have a right to exist as a majority-Jewish state, with Judaism as a state religion? I don't generally object to the existence of Islamic countries (while I may disagree with their policies, as I may with any country of any derivation), so I'd no more object to a Jewish state than I would a Muslim, Christian, or Buddhist state.

There is an issue if Israel, pursuing a colonial, right-wing authoritarian agenda, damaging and devaluing its democracy, wishes to act and expand with particular ideological impetus, occupying or annexing land through violence, and the enforcement of a sort of apartheid is objectionable no matter which state performs it, for any variety of imperial ambition. The distinction between being a majority-Jewish state, or a majority-Christian, Muslim, or Buddhist state, and then that state acting with imperial impetus, is significant. A Jewish or Muslim state does not so essentially need to acquire more land or oppress its neighbours, and it is consistent for any of those entities to not follow imperial, racist, or irredentist aims.

The actions of Hamas are a tragedy, and an expression of evil. The reaction to injustice should not be to augment it. Further besieging Gaza and destroying more lives augments injustice, and as if I need to repeat it again: it is criminal and mistaken.

I'm reminded of Raymond Aron's view (given my sycophancy for the man). A Jew himself, the creation of Israel in 1948 'raised no emotion' for him. Nor was he ever a Zionist, sceptical of the efficacy of any project, being a thoroughly assimilated secular French Jew. He began to take more seriously his Jewish identity (beyond anything said through WW2), when Charles de Gaulle made a famous speech calling Jews "an elite people, self-assured and domineering."

This prompted a book from Aron, and further writing. He didn't wish Israel to be overcome by its enemies and no longer exist, while he recognised that its geographical and geopolitical situation would predictably cause conflict with the Arabs and the Israelis should not be careless (or foolish) in their co-existence. In favour of France's unlikely neutrality in the conflict, his pessimism lead him to define the situation as imprisoned within the violence of the protagonists.

Israel's rightward progression does it no favours, neither does the degrading of its democracy, just as fundamentalism causes any Palestinian political project to self-immolate, as well as provoking immolation by its rivals. Israel appears to have no cogent military strategy in Gaza. The barbarism of Hamas does not free Israel of the responsibility to protect civilian lives in Gaza. Air bombardment, limited incursions, or a full-scale invasion are all bad policies that won't ultimately destroy Hamas, will not ensure the security of Israel, and neither ensure the security of ordinary Palestinians. It is also tactically astute to show the world, when fighting terrorists, that there is a vast moral difference between you and them. In the eyes of many internationally, creating a humanitarian crisis and bombing civilians obscures the difference. Instead, Israel is weakened domestically and internationally. This isn't meant to reject the use of force against Hamas, and the goal of destroying that group is understandable, or even reasonable. The trickier question is how to do this effectively, without the huge cost in life, which even a casual observer can see is not well-analysed. It is unlikely that either side will achieve their strategic objectives.

When Isreal is in the news, or harms more Palestinians, anti-Semitic attacks against Jews internationally increase. Many will be anti-Semitic regardless of what Israel does, even if it conducts itself perfectly, further motivated as well by an appalling act of anti-Jewish terrorism; yet if the only Jewish country in the world is an authoritarian one with a degenerating democracy, pursuing unpopular policies, this is not helpful. One can equally note the rise in Islamophobic violence and hate crimes internationally whenever the Middle East is of greater political priority again, not helped by stereotyped portrayals in news media. To what extent Jews themselves, or anyone else, conflate Jewish identity with Israel is always a fractious discourse, and we can be sympathetic to Jews investing much in Israel, or rejecting its premise and/or policies. Israel does not, and cannot, speak for the whole Jewish diaspora, even if some wish it could, and no country, acknowledging the complexities of identity, can so confidently claim an entire people; and Jews are not a monolithic group of one people. Anti-Semites do not care, and are prone to believing Jews indeed are a monolithic group, and any distinguishing between Jews from Britain, France, Israel, or Uzbekistan, or of any other variance, matters little to them. I am pessimistic enough to believe that it is anti-Semites who designate who Jews are, in the way that matters most. Jews can object, but anti-Semites don't care, and will vandalise Jewish businesses and cemeteries with greater zeal. Jews have to bare the tragedy of lives lost, Palestinians have to endure tragedy; while the state of Israel, Hamas, and their supporters augment it—no solution is yet found, there is no near-future that isn't vile and barbarous, and the result is more dead Israelis and more dead Palestinians.

October 2023

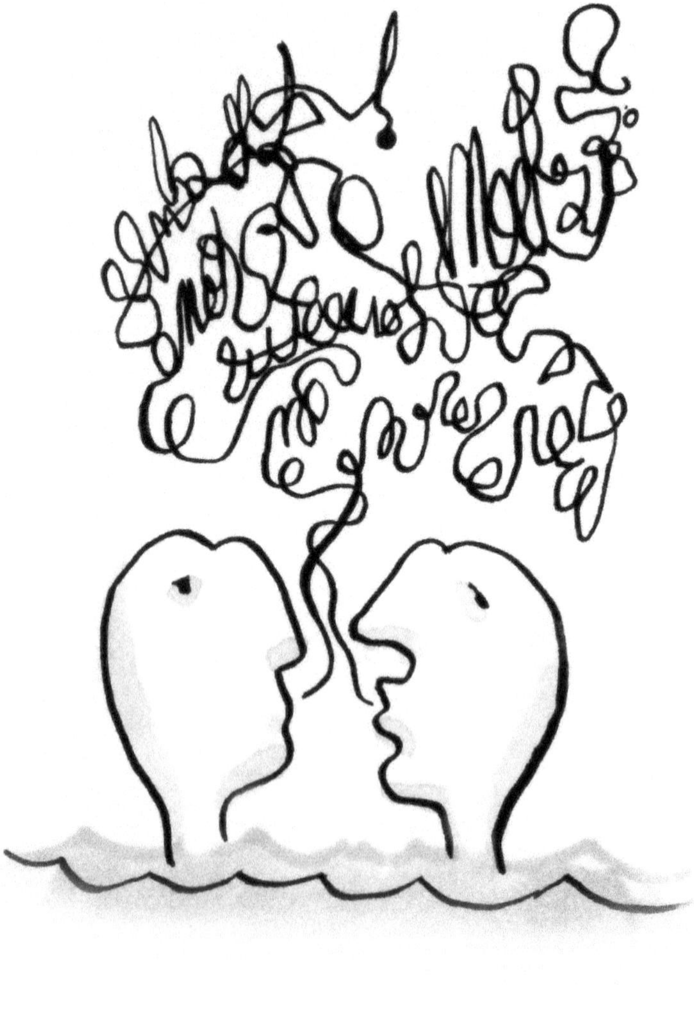

WORDS AND CLARITY

I'M ALMOST FEARFUL of the unwanted connotations so many words possess.

I'm not fond, or rather I am no good at naturally following, rules for *clear* language, apparently unpretentious, not too wordy and complex. So I admit I'm, somehow, posturing and hypocritical. Yet I feel insecure about this, and I really don't think I speaking in some completely obtuse way nobody can understand. Some accuse me of being verbose, but I don't think my vocabulary is very elaborate or outlandish; all the words used here are common and my faults may be with clunky syntax and punctuation. It takes more effort to avoid common metaphors and allusions than to speak robotically, even if I have a problem with convoluted or pretentious metaphors.

I like words, I like words that are not just useful but aesthetically lovely, and I care enough about how I am speaking, and wanting to be understood as well as I can convey, to also equally disdain other words. My autism, as well as the precarious position my illnesses put me in—having to regularly engage with medical professionals—also means that clarity and a fuller understanding of how I am feeling is more important. So I care a lot about how I speak, and I genuinely don't think I speak in some grandiose or overly-complicated way. I find it hard to 'dumb-down' my language, as I've been told I need to do, even if I strive for clarity. I don't think it's difficult to understand what I say, unless I'm over-estimating others.

It's difficult to speak, and especially to explain or identify more complex subjects, without using new-fangled words and evolving vocabulary, and we are often bound within the limits of our language. Much can be said, and has been said, of the limitations of language inhibiting the development of thought or creating its own paradigm; one that can be hard to escape without the introduction of new words and thus a new understanding. Use older vocabulary, and one can appear out-of-touch, offensive (according to current social norms, rightly or wrongly), or fail to adequately describe new developments. New vocabulary is not much better: redundant words in a 're-inventing the wheel' fashion abound, new terms come into use without better definitions and obfuscate things as much as they may, sometimes, bring clarity with the coinage of a pithy phrase, or intuitive description, for a contemporary event or concept.

The fault of older language can be more obvious, and falling into disuse or their failing to properly account for how things have progressed means new words can be useful—at least if the apparent replacement is a robust or accurate descriptor. Though many new words and terms are not good as acute, or even obtuse, descriptors; and my distaste for them can be practical, suggesting that a fashionable phrase doesn't actually give a useful definition, but the other concern is how so many words are *shibboleths*, or in-group signifiers, whose use comes with a great amount of social and cultural baggage. Words are often over-used by different groups with different definitions, many of them ignorant or vulgar. Political vocabulary suffers the worst fate, with too many individual, idiosyncratic, and particular understandings of words by different allegiances, coloured by their prejudices and ideological hankerings. The introduction of so many superfluous words, and the technology to facilitate them, produces more misunderstanding than coherence. Words are now less standardised, a greater democracy of meaning occurs with words, and the reportage of events, with the quantitative expansion of media. One can suggest some, perhaps obvious, moral and practical advantages to advances in literacy. The unintended consequences mean that lies spread faster than truth, with this trend only becoming exaggerated with social media and the internet. An abundance of knowledge, and new words, does not mean we are adept in classifying, understanding, and using them. A larger, disorganised library is worse than a smaller, but organised one.

Even when words are accurate, they can simply be embarrassing in how they sound or how they're used. I don't want to use words that make me cringe because of how aesthetically displeasing they are. Which might seem vain, but I'm not just being petty. Ugly words aren't bad just because they look and sound bad, in some artistic sense; their ugliness creates new connotations, their use by particular people or groups creates new connotations, and eventually the words devolve into clichés and lose meaning in this process—thus becoming less useful or accurate.

Social classes and cultural groups use their own vocabularies and have a great selection of choice words, often adapted and adopted popularly outside their origins. I have a problem with class colloquialisms from all social ranks. Upper and lower classes each use their own language which can be indecipherable to outsiders, and outsiders are then mocked and even punished for failing to understand—if they even had the capacity to do so. This is worse when it's top-down, with cultural elites deriding those they think beneath them for a lack of education or superficial eloquence, yet this doesn't mean lower classes don't perform a similar game, if not as socially and practically damaging. Teenagers mock out-of-touch adults for not knowing the latest cool lingo, and the reverse happens as older generations mock the youth for being ignorant of outmoded phrases and cultural signifiers. Each is guilty of their own sort of hubris. We shouldn't feel a need to mock people for not knowing what many won't even get the time to know. Why should everyone be cognisant of the latest *Fortnite* trend or events occurring years before their birth, entirely irrelevant to their everyday survival?

This is an uncharitable interpretation, and I won't in full sincerity subscribe to it, but I might define this as a sort of cultural hubris, or individualist insecurity where indicating to others that one is part of a specific, insular cultural or social group is, consciously or not, more important than communicating understandably across social and cultural boundaries. I don't entirely begrudge the need, or the desire, for this cultural membership achieved through language, and it's understandable that all of us, besides the most anti-social and misanthropic, act this way. But, ideally, I would want language to function *definitionally*, to describe and explain feelings, processes, ways of being, events, etc, before it is artistic or fashionable. Which is certainly not to say words can't ever be flippant, idiomatic, or silly, but that I have a prioritisation in mind.

The use of words following cultural fashions means less care about being accessible or being understood, and this can be, though not always, somewhat selfish—and worse, creating further barriers and obstacles to understanding each other. If we don't need to really understand each other, the least we should have is an appreciation for other lives, and in its worst configuration unique colloquialisms show a contempt for acknowledging the ignorances of others or making the world, as complex and increasingly fast-paced as it is, more hospitable. If a new word obfuscates our understanding of something more than it defines it effectively, then on balance it's not a good word—even if it sounds good to say or follows a recent trend. I think a collective coherence of words is more important than words following fashions, changing with the wind and acting as *signifiers* before, more neutrally, serving a practical function of conveying information and knowledge. Which should not be essential, but at least a decent suggestion.

This does not mean we can, or should, develop some way of speaking and writing that, in some bland, impossibly-objective process, serves a pure functionality or aligns to some narrow *prescriptivism*. I am not a prescriptivist, solid in some conviction of the definition of words, and I fully accept the premise, or actuality, that the meaning of words comes more from their use and the context of their use; and I am fine to use nouns as verbs or turn adjectives into verbs, or the opposite, and frequently change the meaning and context of words in a perpetually evolving process, socially, for comedy, or just in my own idiosyncratic use. The more pertinent concern, whether one subscribes to a theory of linguistics where definitions and use are prescribed or described, is the efficacy of words and definitions. It is good to change the meaning of words, especially if an earlier use is less comprehensible than a modern understanding, and I think my overly-critical, discerning use of words doesn't mean I'm any sort of language purist. The opposite is true, I'm far closer to Lewis Carroll and *"when I use a word . . . it means just what I choose it to mean—neither more nor less"*. I'm just more pedantically concerned about the ability to be understood, or rather have my meaning not be so easily lost and confused—even if I don't think a true understanding is possible. It's a matter of survival and my good health that I express myself in a way that isn't easily misunderstood.

Trying to police and enforce language more actively, with official or organised interventions, will produce much greater problems and lead to significant misunderstanding, trying to control what we can't or shouldn't artificially control. Speaking differently is not a crime. And I know my personal concerns are just that: personal, and my complaints mean little. I do not intend to be the Word Police. I'm not making a serious, or practicable, call to action, policy instruction, or asking that others, somehow, alter their speech to fit my peculiar tastes. Nor do I, really, discredit the use of all euphemisms and I enjoy a fun turn-of-phrase. I use eccentric or particular phrases and names all the time that others, seeking some distilled clearest version of English, would think are niche and require too much explanation or prior knowledge. I still hold some minor contention, on balance, that contemporary society has further proliferated, and at greater speed, words that don't, first, fulfil the purpose of providing a clear definition and eliminating misunderstandings as much as we can. And better words exist.

There isn't a good way to solve this, creating my own special and unique language and lexicon brings just as much, if not more trouble—so the very least I try to do is limit (though never eliminate) the use of esoteric, jargon nouns, and describe things in as straightforward a way as I can, limiting the use of euphemisms unless I'm trying to be funny or unserious.

Some of this article is prompted by a funny post I made in an online *meme* group, insincerely, jokingly, partly as a self-parody and hinting at my own autistic, obsessive fixation with perceptions and appearances:

> I hate all neologisms, buzzwords, shibboleths, euphemisms, clichés, jargon, colloquialisms, lingo, and trendy nomenclature, associated with any subculture, because I am unique and special.
>
> Instead of using neologisms, buzzwords, shibboleths, euphemisms, clichés, jargon, colloquialisms, lingo, and trendy nomenclature, I prefer to describe and explain things with more detailed definitions while not so easily resorting to neologisms, buzzwords, shibboleths, euphemisms, clichés, jargon, colloquialisms, lingo, and trendy nomenclature that require further explanation or shared, implicit understandings others may not possess.
>
> If I really must use any neologisms, buzzwords, shibboleths, euphemisms, clichés, jargon, colloquialisms, lingo, or trendy nomenclature, for ease, 'shorthand', or convenience, I do so in quotations and with an eye-roll (🙄), sarcastically, or as a joke. This is because I am smarter than you, and better than you, and I don't wish to be associated with any groups.
>
> Any groups that I appear to be a part of are blessed with my presence only for the purposes of research, or I am only a constituent of various taxonomical, political, social, cultural, familial, or geographical groupings involuntarily.

Regardless, that's why Joe Biden is *Goated with the sauce* and is a *Sigma Chad* with *W Rizz* for supporting the unions.

October 2023

LEMONS

LEMONS WAS my best friend. With my health being so poor, and feeling miserable so often, Lemons was my reliable companion and I loved him in ways I struggle to write.

He would follow me everywhere around the house. Late at night, if I got up to get a drink or go to the toilet, he'd always follow me to the bathroom just to be near me. He would wander up to me when I'd return home and want me to follow him upstairs, or he'd greet me with affectionate licks and snuggles. I was the only person he allowed to really hold and cuddle him. If he was outside and heard me call him, or just moving around, he'd quickly rush inside to see me. He had various spots around the house he'd love to sleep in: at the bottom of my bed, on the green bean-bag, the cushion on my chair at the kitchen table if you didn't move it away. His food is still in my room; his special diet for his kidneys, and I'd hear him almost every night walking into my room to eat and play with the scratching posts—before jumping onto my bed. He would meow loudly when the dogs were being fed their medication, as he knew he'd get a treat. You could hear him walking around the house as the little bell on his collar would jingle. He always knew if you opened a tuna can or got ham from the fridge, and would rush to be beside you. He loved attention and would meekly paw at you to stroke him and give him affection.

But he's gone now.

He was sick on my birthday, and looked lethargic and dehydrated, so we took him to the vets in the evening to have fluids and make sure he was okay. He was fine the night before and looked normal that morning. But he deteriorated, and died in the evening on the 13th. We went to see him at the vets, to be with him, and sadly there was nothing they could do—so we had to say goodbye.

He likely ingested something poisonous, after a malicious intervention from a neighbour. I will not elaborate on that in case of any legalities.

I am lost without Lemons. Grief is the most effecting and significant emotion, all others fail to compare in their hold over a person or their impact. Grief is from love; it takes advantage of positive notions, of beauty, of any typical lust for life and happiness, in the gross magnification of misery. No trick truly dispels it. It creeps and returns. It might become more hospitable with time, but the stereotypical stages of grief are a scheme—to try and grasp it—that fail to note its real shifts and oscillations, its coming and going, its subtleties and its upheavals. It's the emotion, or set of feelings, we most fail to properly contend with. There are incorrect ways to grieve, that are destructive or harmful, but there aren't any correct ways either. Some better than others, always dependent and individual, always a new unknown. Everything is so scary.

I am so grateful to Lemons. He made me less afraid of life. He was happiness and joy, and with him I could forget bad things for a while.

I love you, always.

I value materiality. I value blood and flesh and biology. Physicality, objects, tactile feelings, skin, physiology.

Excess materialism is a joke as it doesn't value objects, small and precious possessions; it disposes of the old and moves onwards to the next fashion. Immateriality holds no greater emotional value for me, it offers no respite, no peace, no love, no sadness nor weeping. Its unsatisfying character is hard for me to overstate. Becoming one with the universe as a dispersed consciousness is also unfulfilling, as are other arcane or esoteric precepts—if it's even possible for us to reckon with them reasonably, and in a way that remains human.

My intellectual considerations, what I think of cosmology, metaphysics, or epistemology, aren't anything I find solace in. They're primitive, cold, amoral, with no concern for human or animal feeling. I would prefer to consider my feelings. I want a fleshy reunion even after my decay and entropy, bound to material sensations, meeting dead pets and friends again. I'll prefer a cartoonish idea of an afterlife—emotionally, if not rationally or intellectually—to what I know of common canon texts and beliefs on the matter; which if they aren't denials of death's reality, their versions of life beyond earth are too obscure, aloof, and dubious. Earthly sensations are deemed lesser to divine ones, in a few dominant teachings, but divine sensations are nothing to me.

There are versions of afterlife that do include, in literal detail, what I'd desire; but I have no way to access them without feeling lied to, or as if I'm participating in a comforting delusion.

I still can't find myself agreeing with a better vision of death: I'm prevented by a cold cynicism that suggests annihilation is more probable and real than my dreams or others' consolatory stories.

I am passionately a sensualist, but never too much. I value what I can touch and what causes me, in my fragile body, to cry in joy or in grief. I know too much of physical pain, a permanent state of scratching irritation and inflammation, though I'd never want to eliminate it; which would be alien. I do not value pain, especially for any vulgar artistic of pedagogical purposes, yet life without any experience of it would be more callous, more dismissive, and with less sympathy. The elimination of disease and disability is a utopian aim and I have little time for such hubris. I'm caused to value the tactile and sensual over much else. The feel of hair, tastes, smells. I disdain machismo, masochism, and the pursuit of pain: a perversion. Nor do I value excess hedonism: another perversion. I cherish tender moments of physicality that aren't paramount (or are dismissed in favour of higher concepts) in austere spiritualisms or denials of life and death.

I value nature, wildlife, flora, and I don't appreciate dogmas that do away with it. But I wish, against nature, that even if I and my friends decay I could somehow be preserved without losing my physical essence. I think this is impossible, and I hold no belief in the existence of an afterlife with preserved consciousness. But this is unfortunate and I hope for my own reasoning is flawed. I don't appreciate religious dogma and have no desire whatsoever to have any sort of union or sanctuary with a higher power—or at least as they're described by the dominant religious metaphysics, or Abrahamic mythology. I just want love and the preservation of very animal feelings, in some magical realm where I can meet my cat again, maybe converse with dead thinkers and friends, and enjoy good food and drink. This is certainly not an uncommon desire, so I wish it were so. It's such a common desire that many of the spiritually-inclined make their own dogma to include it, even when it's not present in scripture. Others suggest a diffused consciousness or soul disseminated across the universe after death, which I find just as bleak as total annihilation into non-existence. I don't wish to be inhuman.

There is a metaphysics suggested by the concept of the *Rainbow Bridge*. Its origins are unclear, as far as I know, from a poem published in the 1980s, suggesting that when a beloved pet dies, they cross the rainbow bridge into an afterlife full of the many joys a cat, dog, bird, or other pet would enjoy. But you, their human companion, are not there with them. Eventually, one day, you will die too and cross the same rainbow bridge. Your pet is waiting and they are delighted to see you, they rush towards you and lick you or snuggle you or do whatever they're capable of doing to display affection. This reunion, even when described in saccharine detail, is more satisfying and comforting than the entirety of Christian dogma on the nature of death and Heaven. What can anyone say of death? We are no smarter than the ancient Greeks or ancient Jews; while wealthier in information and experiences we make no fewer mistakes, in our personal lives or in political action. On death, we have the same mixture of "sentimental or stoically-moderated emotional effusions."* Feeble protests, verbose consolations, and all the same uncontrolled rumours of immortality and eternal life. I'm rude enough to find none of it satisfying. I don't care for God or most described in scripture, I just want my friend.

October 2023

---

*from *Until My Eyes Are Closed With Shards* (1977)—Manès Sperber

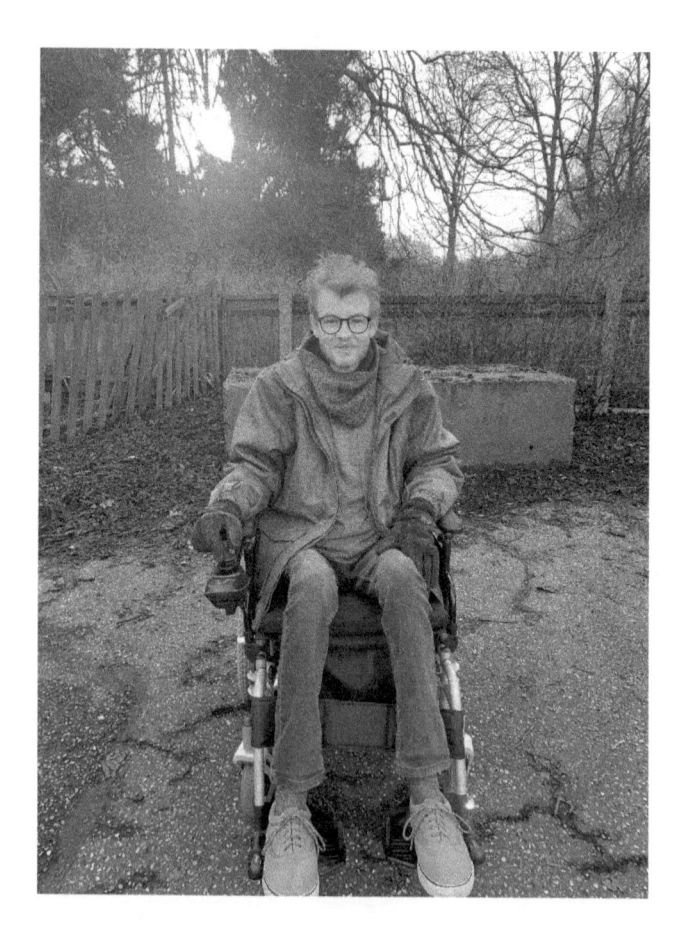

Jake Goldsmith is a writer with cystic fibrosis and the founder of The Barbellion Prize, a book prize for ill and disabled authors. He is the author of *Neither Weak Nor Obtuse* (Sagging Meniscus, 2022) and a contributing editor to *Exacting Clam*.

Wend Rend is a disabled artist from Portland, OR. She holds an MA in Critical Theory and Creative Research from the Pacific Northwest College of Art. Wend focuses on embodied analog approaches to psychoanalytic art and cognitive rehabilitation. Her ongoing semiotic research project is titled Monstrorum Historia, and can be found on Patreon.